EMBODYING YOUR SOUL

EMBODYING YOUR SOUL

A Detailed Guide for Merging with Your Higher Self and the Absolute

Fernando A. Obando

Copyright © 2022 by Fernando A. Obando

Email: Embodying_Your_Soul@yahoo.com

All rights reserved. No part of this publication may be reproduced, distributed, or transmitted in any form or by any means, including photocopying, recording, or other electronic or mechanical methods, without the prior written permission of the publisher, except in the case of brief quotations embodied in critical reviews and certain other noncommercial uses permitted by copyright law.

The author of this book does not present medical or psychological advice or prescribe the use of any technique or exercise, directly or indirectly, as a form of treatment for any medical or psychological problem without the advice of a physician or physiologist. The intent of the author is to provide information to encourage inner spiritual growth and attainment to enhance our relation within the Universe. In the event that you use any of the information in this book, you do so at your own discretion. The author assumes no responsibility for any adverse effect or consequences resulting from the use of the information, practices or techniques described in this book.

Editorial consultation: Stephanie Gunning

Hardcover ISBN: 978-1-7780252-1-1

Paperback ISBN: 978-1-7780252-0-4

Digital ISBN: 978-1-7780252-2-8

1st edition, January 2022

Contents

Introduction

Part One: The Search for Knowledge and the Self

Chapter 1: Reality and the Self   9

Chapter 2: The Three Centers of the Soul   15

Chapter 3: The Two Links   27

Chapter 4: The Stages of Self-Realization   31

Chapter 5: The Mystery of Solitude   41

Part Two: The Self-Realization of Personality

Chapter 6: Beyond Personality   49

Chapter 7: Becoming a Self-Aware Observer   53

Chapter 8: Becoming a Conscious Observer   59

Part Three: The Self-Realization of Individuality

Chapter 9: The Quest for the Soul   65

Chapter 10: Stabilization of the Mental Body   69

Chapter 11: Awakening the Ethereal Body   83

Chapter 12: Awakening the Emotional Body   103

Chapter 13: Awakening the Mental Body   143

Chapter 14: Unification of the Three Centers of the Soul

Part Four: The Self-Realization of Universality

Chapter 15: The Quest for the Absolute   157

Chapter 16: Surrendering Awareness and Liberation 163

Chapter 17: Merging into the Universal Source   169

Chapter 18: Integration of Samadhi Within Daily Life

List of Diagrams   181

List of Practices   183

References   185

About the Author   189

INTRODUCTION

The book you are about to read is a compilation of information gleaned from many years of practice and study in the area of spirituality and meditation.

Although I've studied spirituality and practiced meditation for most of my life, through the eyes of most professionals in this field my educational credentials are not clearly established. I have worked as a professional engineer and project manager. It wasn't until 2013 that I decided to phase out my involvement with engineering and dedicate more time and focus to my spiritual evolution. I traveled to India and participated in various retreats for several years, including secluding myself for long periods to meditate. This was when I had the opportunity to concentrate on my spiritual path and embody my soul.

Over the course of a seven-year period, I experienced a range of changes in my personality. As a consequence, I am no longer the person I was before except for having the ability to hold in mind memories of my departed past at different ages. I do not consider myself a seeker of reality anymore; however, I still continue practicing meditation.

Throughout my life, I've collected and analyzed material from different traditions. Now I've also compiled an outline of the processes I consider essential to exploring the inner self and merging with the soul and the absolute. Like many who have heard the same call, I felt drawn to the subject by a force so persistent I could not ignore it.

I firmly believe that all my experiences as a practicing meditator, together with those I have collected from other practitioners I've encountered, will greatly help you. If you are ready to embody your soul and drawn to connect to the absolute, then consider this book an opportunity to explore the path of spiritual knowledge and practices that will make this possible.

My intent in writing this book is to provide you with all the information you need to access your inner dimensions and support your soul's evolution. It contains detailed information on how to remember your true nature, and most importantly, it will help you to expand into the infinite realms of the universal self.

Having said all this, in my opinion this book is not for the masses. Rather, it is likely to appeal to those who have reached a certain degree of spiritual development and want to recognize their existence beyond the mere psychological contents of their physical, emotional, and mental bodies.

By reading this book, novice meditation practitioners will encounter a complete route to enter and explore the confines of their inner dimensions. If you are a novice, perhaps this will speed you along the path. Advanced practitioners will get a clearer picture of the same route through in-depth clarification about the different stages of the evolution into the soul and how, sooner or later, they will have the ability to access and merge with the absolute. Everybody does. The path is universal.

The *absolute* is a term used to signify the dimension of the source or the uncreated. It also indicates the realm of absence.

Although the book uses modern terminology, it has its foundations in ancient spiritual traditions. Nevertheless, you won't find the content merely to be a repetition of the same teachings published by other teachers. In writing it, I deliberately avoided duplicating old parables and borrowing antique language, and instead provided practical descriptions of actual experiences about how to enter and explore your inner dimensions. I have done my best to avoid overlaying it with the morality and traditions of any particular culture or religion.

At its base, the soul's intrinsic nature demands freedom. Even so, it is interesting to see how many people think the spiritual path is described perfectly by scriptures dating back to antiquity. Many firmly believe there is nothing else to add. The reality is that, as sacred and important as those old scriptures are, we cannot continue adhering to their precepts without clarifying what they mean.

It is my contention in this book that we need to see the world from a different perspective—from a universal point of view. Spirituality is independent of religion because our spiritual evolution primarily comes from our inner dimension. No external religious intermediary or institutional affiliation is able to duplicate or drive it.

How This Book Is Organized

Within this book, you will find different chapters explaining in detail how to acquire self-realization at the spiritual level. The initial chapters include basic concepts that are necessary to understand the material in the later sections of the book.

I have divided the evolutionary spiritual process into three aspects: the self-realization of personality, the self-realization of individuality, and the self-realization of universality. In Part One, I give an overview of all the elements of the journey, including the importance of solitude and a detailed explanation of the three centers of the soul that must be activated in order for you to call in your soul.

These three aspects of the journey to embody your soul include the turning points through which we, as human beings, have the opportunity to evolve during our lives. At each threshold, we have the opportunity to evolve into new states of consciousness.

Part Two, on the self-realization of personality, describes the process of becoming aware of our real identity—the true self—and the awakening of higher awareness.

Part Three, on the self-realization of individuality, describes the process for the purification of the ethereal, emotional, and mental bodies. This is an essential step in the practice of spirituality. The ability to purify ourselves is a critical capacity that enables us to embody our souls.

While learning the practices that make the self-realization of individuality possible in this phase, many people have doubts about the value of going further. To embody the soul, we need to be willing to surrender everything we are. Practitioners may feel afraid of surrendering the most important treasures of their human existence—those things by which they define themselves to themselves. It is only those who have spiritually evolved enough that are ready to cross this threshold and experience.

Part Four, the final section of the book, covers the self-realization of universality, which is the main purpose of our existence. Living as a universal being in unity with the soul and the absolute is the highest level of spiritual evolution that we can attain as human beings. Here, I explain how to become a master of wisdom within the light of creation directly operating from your soul.

There are different ways of reading this book. You may feel confident enough with your spiritual knowledge and personal practice to browse portions of the book, or you may benefit more from reading it from beginning to end while exploring the different exercises and maintaining a daily meditation practice. Either way is perfectly acceptable.

While I suggest a sequential reading of the book, I can understand why more experienced practitioners might wish to skip ahead or around. No matter how much work on ourselves any of us has done, it is important to recognize that trying to practice or enter into advanced dimensions of consciousness is only possible if we have completed the necessary steps and requirements, as described in the initial chapters of this book.

The process of awakening that I have written about in this book is a synthesis of my interpretations of my own experiences on the spiritual path and interpretations of the path that other meditation practitioners shared with me. I hope it helps you navigate your own journey of evolving into your soul.

Again, I emphasize that the purpose of this book is to facilitate the self-discovery of your inner dimensions. Reading the book and simply taking my word for the nature of the spiritual path is not going to be sufficient to embody your soul and merge with the absolute; you will have to put in some effort to experience these things for yourself. Practicing meditation is the best prescription for discovering the hidden dimensions of the soul.

PART ONE

THE SEARCH FOR KNOWLEDGE AND THE SELF

Chapter 1

REALITY AND THE SELF

The way we see the world is largely the result of shared beliefs, attitudes, and ideas drawn from a collective society. We learn to see ourselves as individuals with names, bodies, and values that the societies of our origins have defined.

During our early years, our familial, cultural, and social environments provide us with information about who we are. As we grow and relate to others, our interactions with the outside world also contribute to having a certain view of our existence. Because of experiencing our physiological needs, we are likely to place more importance on the physical world than on our souls, overlooking the soul in our development of our self-images.

As we evolve, we learn about life through collective experiences that expand our knowledge and social skills. By interacting with others, each of us gets an impression of being an individual represented by a name and a physical body. This is how we acquire the information that generates the attributes, behavior, and responses that form our personalities.

Throughout childhood, our view of reality adjusts to the external factors that affect our lives, defining how we relate to the world and people around us. While growing within a collective consciousness context, we reach certain degree of mental and emotional maturity.

After a certain period of time, but usually in adulthood, most of us begin asking questions about reality. We start wondering if we have erroneous perceptions about reality, perhaps based on distorted beliefs or faulty information.

During this quest for knowledge, this reality test, we may investigate different spiritual teachings. We check here and there for the truth and then, finally, appreciate that teachings can only provide us with a guide to finding our answers; they are not a substitute for our own experience of reality. If we want to discover the nature of reality, we cannot continue searching for it outside us. We need to look for that truth within because it is in there that we find the interpretation for our reality.

Through self-reflection, we may develop an appreciation of who we are, what our beliefs are, and, in general, why we think, feel, and act as we do. Self-reflection is an exercise that uses the information from our surrounding world to understand the qualities that exist inside us.

By practicing self-reflection, the "self" initially perceives the world as a mirror image of its own consciousness, a source of meaning and definition. It is for this reason that the self represents our reality and vehicle for interpreting our existence.

Since our understanding of the self depends subjectively on the reference we give it, it can be based either on the mind or on the soul (or anything else we pay attention to) in our self-reflection process. At the most basic level, the self refers to the experience of the observer established by placing our attention on the mind. From the perspective of an advanced consciousness, however, the self holds the sense of "I am" that comes from the soul.

The mind always needs a frame of reference to define reality while the soul does not need any reference or relationship to register it. Interpretations of reality depend on how we process our perceptions. Each of us has a different view of reality and referencing ourselves. What is true for one may not be true for others; however, the perception will only be universally true if it reflects the soul.

For instance, if you ask, "Who am I?" your answer could be, "I am a father, a mother, a husband, a wife, an engineer, an accountant," and so forth. As we can see, these answers are the result of how you are related to people or what you do. You are a husband because you have a spouse. Or you are a mother because you have children. Or you are an engineer because you design, build, or, in general, have the knowledge to practice engineering.

Your mind provides these answers based on your relationships and roles in the external world. Your ways of defining your identity are different from the ways others define themselves because of your individual circumstances and theirs. If we did not define ourselves within a frame of reference, we simply would not be able to answer this question. The mind believes we would not exist or have any meaning.

Obviously, this type of answer is incomplete and does not encompass our entire essence.

When we include our soul in the same process without making any comparisons or relying upon references to roles and functions, we can get a universal response to the question "Who am I?" It may seem strange or be hard to believe, but the soul does not need a frame of reference to interpret reality because it is eternal and resides in a different dimension. From there, it provides our real identity and becomes the essence of our real self.

As you read this book, you may observe how the perspective of the self that is having the experience I am describing will shift. If this gets confusing, please remember that I am always writing from the perspective of the level of consciousness being discussed in that particular chapter.

Reality within the physical dimension is relative and changes depending on time and space. For this reason, today we are someone, and tomorrow we can be someone different. The interpretation of reality is temporary because we confine it to our mental and emotional experience of the physical dimension.

The dimension of the soul is not relative because it dwells in the void of the uncreated. Therefore, the soul is eternal and never changes. *Absolute* is another way of saying "not relative."

We are human beings inhabiting a transient, changeable physical world. Our true selves, however, are based on the energy of the soul whose energy is pure consciousness. At the level of soul, we are neither bodies nor products of our minds. Rather, we are consciousness.

Many people restrict their self-knowledge to the reality obtained from the external world without questioning the fundamentals of their existence. Unaware of their souls, they suppress their natural way of being and rely on false representations to define them. They do not have a sense of true identity because they are disconnected from their souls. Their souls are not yet embodied.

They do not yet realize that life in the body is a temporary stage of an eternal existence, or that we are here mainly for the purpose of transcending our human condition—not to spend our whole lives refining it.

Your soul is "out there" for you; however, you might as well not have a soul until you actually experience it. Having a link with your soul is not as simple as repeating the mantra "I am a soul" or saying, "I am not this body." The first step of the self-realization process is realizing your real and eternal identity as separate from your physical body.

Your main goal of spiritual practice, initially, should be to understand how you interpret your reality and make the necessary adjustments to experience your soul. Making an assessment of the status of your reality and improving your self-knowledge is a good starting point to bring your personality under control.

After developing your understanding of how you interpret your reality, you can start building a link to your soul by exploring your inner dimensions and recognizing the three centers of the soul.

Chapter 2

THE THREE CENTERS OF THE SOUL

Our initial perception of the self emerges from the five senses of the physical body and yet it is based on the energy of the ethereal, emotional, and mental aspects of our world. These three components, therefore, are the foundation of the human psychological structure known as the *personality*.

The physical component is the densest of the four components. This component encompasses all the elements of creation.

The ethereal component of the human energy field is an exact replica and counterpart of the physical component, and it is within this component that we can perceive the flow of energy that sparks life. The receptor for ethereal energy is the center of our feelings, which is located in the lower abdomen.

The emotional component of the human energy field flows in through the center of the physical body up to the heart level from whence it distributes itself to all parts of the body. The receptor of emotional energy is located in the chest.

Finally, to complete the list of three components of the human psychological structure, we have the mental component. The receptor of mental energy is located in the head. Mental energy dominates the human experience and empowers us to be self-reflective.

Evolution of the ethereal, emotional, and mental "bodies" brings our psyches into a more advanced system. We could say that this system is the purified energetic portion of the initial three components.

In the context of our bodies, these energy receptors are the centers of the soul because it is through them that we may build the links we need to access and embody our souls. For the remainder of this book, we will call them *centers of the soul* or *soul centers*.

Most eastern spiritual traditions agree that the centers of the soul function as portals where individual energy and spiritual consciousness interact to allow for the evolution of the self.

The three soul centers are like buckets of water, and they hold energy particles with different densities. Among the three, the ethereal body contains the densest particles. The emotional body holds subtler particles. The mental holds particles of the lowest density. Or, in other words, the subtlest particles.

Different traditions around the world recognize the centers of the soul in their teachings. For instance, esoteric traditions consider them as centers of energy and consciousness: the head (mental body), the chest (emotional body), and the belly (ethereal body) or vehicles. Some eastern traditions talk about them as the upper, middle, and lower *tan tien*.

Although the chakra system is more widely known than the centers of the soul system, both the Taoist and Vedic traditions locate the chakras within the scope of all three of these soul centers.

While traditions of East and West use different identification systems for them, we can recognize that various models and conventions are referring to the same energetic areas in the body.

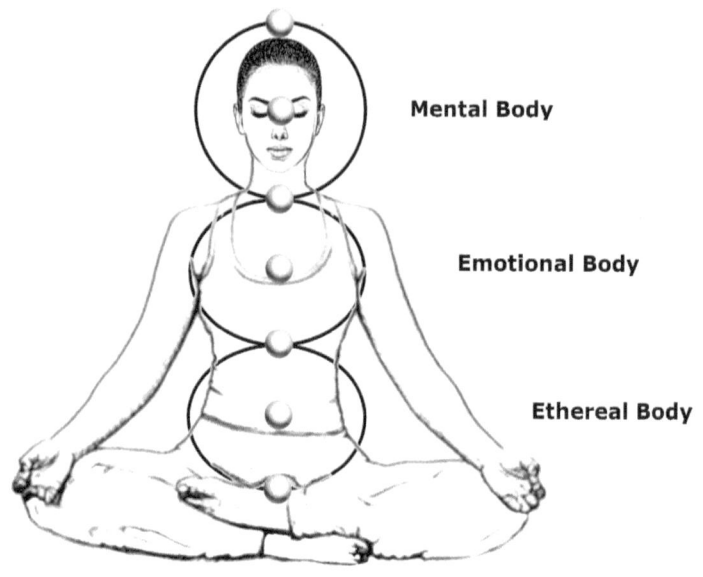

THE THREE SOUL CENTERS

The Ethereal Body

The ethereal body is the energetic image of the physical body. The portal to access this center is situated within the abdomen, an area that is the center of vital energy and physical awareness.

The portal of the ethereal soul center is located within the abdomen. The lowest point of this soul center is the perineum, which is the location of the root chakra. The middle portion of the ethereal soul center is comprised of both the navel and the acupressure point known as the *ming men,* respectively called the front and back gates of the spleen chakra.

The top of this soul center is located in the solar plexus chakra, where it serves as a gate for the exchange of energy between the ethereal and emotional bodies.

The three chakras that are located within the ethereal body are the root, spleen, and solar plexus chakras.

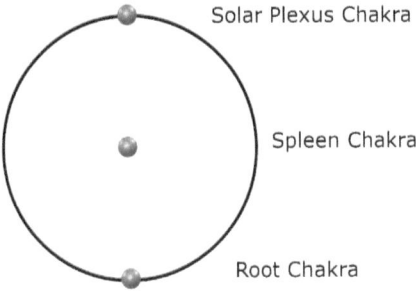

Ethereal Body

The Emotional Body

The soul center associated with the emotional body is located in the chest. As well as the center of emotions, it functions as the doorway to the divine dimension and the essence of the soul.

The top of this center is located at the base of the throat, which is the location of the throat chakra. This uppermost point serves as a bridge for an exchange of energy between the emotional body and the mental body.

The bottom of the emotional soul center is just below the rib cage, which corresponds to the location of the solar plexus chakra. As we've discussed, this chakra serves as a bridge to the ethereal body. The middle point of the emotional soul center is located in the chest and contains the heart chakra.

The three chakras located within the emotional body are the solar plexus, heart, and throat chakras.

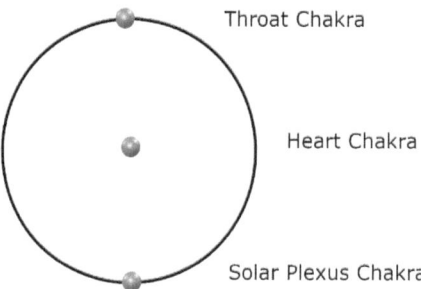

Emotional Body

The Mental Body

The mental soul center is located in the head and its field of energy is the mind. It functions as a portal to universal consciousness and the "I am" consciousness of the soul.

The uppermost point of the mental soul center is on the top of the head and corresponds to the access point of the crown chakra.

The middle of the soul center is at the level of the pineal gland and known colloquially as the *third eye*—the sixth chakra.

The lowest point of the mental soul center is just below the head and corresponds to the throat chakra.

The three physical energy centers that are located within the mental body are the throat, third eye, and crown chakras.

Mental Body

- Crown Chakra
- Third Eye Chakra
- Throat Chakra

The Dimensions of the Soul Within Our Bodies

The human energy field contains the subtle energy of the physical, ethereal, emotional, and ethereal bodies. We can perceive energy from different dimensions of reality according to the level of our spiritual evolution. Each of our soul centers is a vehicle that allows us to shift from one dimension of perception into another. After we recognize each of these centers, we can purify it and master it to evolve our souls. This process is known as *awakening*.

During awakening, we learn of the existence of a new dimension by accessing the corresponding center of the soul. As we advance and get familiar with the qualities and functions of each soul center, we can move into a new and more advanced dimension of reality.

We begin awakening by exploring the ethereal dimension. After mastering this, we can access and explore the emotional dimension. And after that, we can purify and explore the mental dimension. As we progress, the focus of our attention rises through these dimensions.

Remember, we define ourselves by what we focus on. You'll observe that I am giving the "self" a new name at each level of spiritual evolution in order to distinguish the perceptions. We go from identifying with the physical body to identifying with the soul, with different stops in between.

The word *dimension* refers to different configurations of energy, various conditions through which we experience reality. Some people call them planes of existence or planes of reality. Some call them worlds of existence.

The physical, ethereal, emotional, and mental dimensions of our existence are the foundation of everything that has a meaning to us according to our perception.

The physical dimension is solidly material and, for that reason, considered the densest. The ethereal dimension is much less dense than the physical. Even subtler are the emotional and mental dimensions.

When working with ethereal energy, you will experience it as being like a liquid running throughout your ethereal body.

Continuing the analogy to water, the experience of the emotional energy is similar to experiencing water vapor emerging from the emotional body.

The experience of mental energy within the mental body is similar to being submerged into an ocean of expanding spaciousness that turns into clarity or transparency when entering the absolute.

Shifting from one dimension to another is directly proportional to vibration. In fact, each of the chakras or portals of the soul vibrates according to a specific pitch on the chromatic scale. If we want to go to higher dimensions, the frequency of our vibration must be elevated.

The dimensions of reality are superimposed on one another. I like to visualize them as concentric spheres with the highest being the most expansive. When trying to cross between dimensions, we arrive at the vibratory equivalent of a security gate. We can only pass through by creating the right conditions. Those conditions dictate if we can shift to the next level.

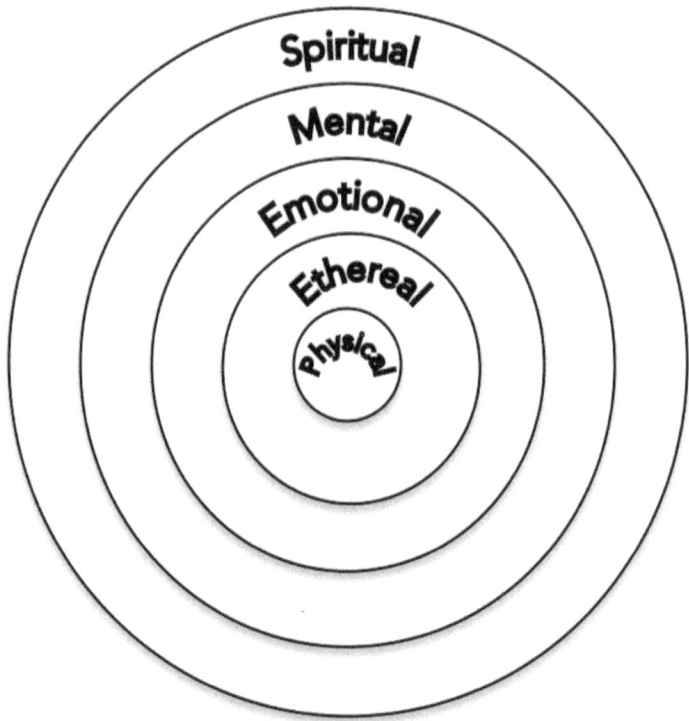

DIMENSIONS OF REALITY

The chakras exchange energy among themselves, always looking to establish equilibrium of the three centers of the soul. They also act as energy gateways or energy exchange from and out of our inner energetic field. The root chakra exchanges vital energy with the creation, the crown chakra exchanges the energy of consciousness with the soul and the universal source. The other chakras function as portals of the three centers of the soul, more specifically the solar plexus and throat chakras transfer energy with the surrounding world.

Although the three centers of the soul are located in different areas of the body, the ethereal, emotional, and mental bodies surround the physical body and encompass its contours. Their energy is more expansive than the soul centers and they are superimposed on one another similar to the picture of "Dimensions of Reality" shown in page 24.

Chapter 3

THE TWO LINKS

The process of merging with the soul and later with the absolute primarily requires us to recognize two flows of energy that continuously regulate our existence in the physical dimension: the flows of consciousness and vital energy. Unless we acknowledge our links to these two flows, evolving into our souls is impossible. Our quest would be as futile as trying to go someplace without knowing its location.

If you decide you want to recognize these two flows, you have to do it by entering your energetic inner dimensions in meditation. There is a detailed explanation of this process in Chapter 6, "The Self-Realization of Personality."

The first flow of energy or link to our soul connects us with consciousness. This is the illumination of the soul that allows us to be aware of our true identity. Consciousness flows from the soul directly into the mental body, where it has an influence over the emotional and physical bodies. As we evolve, we eventually recognize this flow as a sense of awareness.

The second flow of energy we need to locate is the link to the flow of our vital energy. This is the energy that enables us to be alive in the physical dimension. The force of creation emits raw vital energy, which we then receive through the abdominal soul center associated with our ethereal bodies, from which it is distributed throughout our physical bodies.

Vital energy has the capacity to spark life. It is the energy that allows seeds to germinate and keeps all organisms alive. All living beings are linked to this flow, so if their connection to it gets blocked, or the flow is somehow disrupted, they die.

Accepting the existence of these two links and the two flows of energy that come through them into our bodies is only the first step to mastering these energies. We need to learn how to perceive them, yes, but it is also more important to understand how to use them to evolve into our souls.

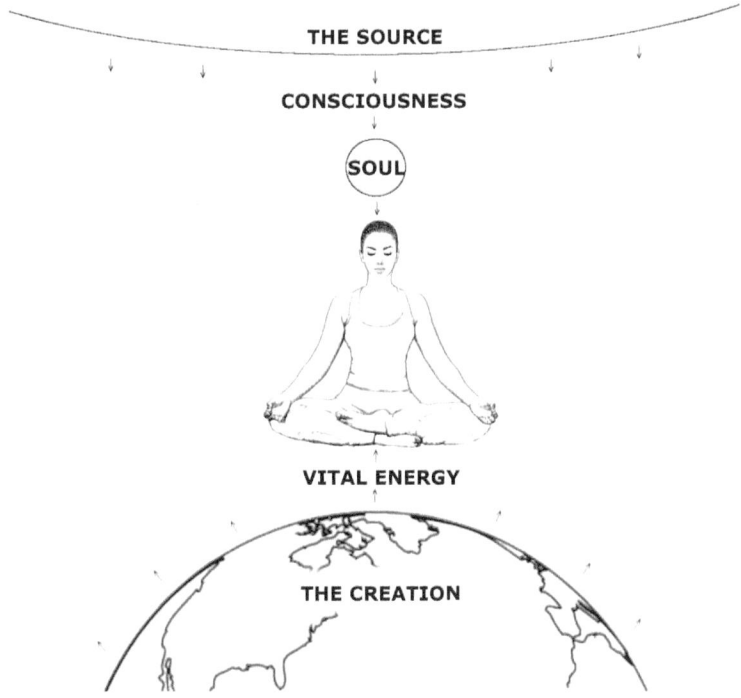

THE LINKS TO CONSCIOUSNESS AND VITAL ENERGY

Once you have acknowledged the gateways for the flow of consciousness and vital energy, and can sense their flowing presence in you, the doors to your spiritual evolution will begin to open for you. At this point, you won't feel isolated anymore and your life may take on real meaning. These two energies allow us to think and live.

To reiterate, our initial task in meditation is to recognize the flow of these two types of energy into the body. Subsequently, and perhaps more importantly, our task is to use them to establish a link to the soul and the ultimate source of creation: the absolute.

Strengthening this deeper connection is the main goal of spiritual evolution.

Chapter 4

THE STAGES OF SELF-REALIZATION

Within this chapter, I will summarize the necessary stages to establish a deeper connection to the source of creation so we may evolve and make space for the soul. Here, I am introducing concepts that initially can be difficult to grasp. If this is the case for you, please make a note to revisit them later. Each of the stages described will be further explained within a dedicated chapter.

Before we go further, let's take a quick look at each of the three stages of self-realization in order.

Stage 1: The Self-Realization of Personality

The first stage, the self-realization of personality, is the recognition of our real identity, as a soul. In this stage, we are detecting a primary spark of light from the soul reflected in our mind.

This is the initial step that must occur because the light of the soul is the energy that will guide us throughout the rest of our spiritual evolution.

Before this initial stage, we may accept the existence of the soul or the possibility of connecting to it only in theory. We do not actually sense the existence of the soul within yet. But it is not enough to have just a theoretical knowledge of its existence to progress. We will need to experience its presence.

The idea that our souls have always been with us is somehow acceptable; however, it is clear that the soul does not exist until we actually recognize it. If we are not capable of identifying or sensing the soul, it does not exist. It simply is not there for us.

We need to prepare our bodies and, in general, our personalities so that we are able to attune to the dimension of the soul and perceive its illumination. This is the first step in building our connection to the soul that will allow us to evolve and embody it, and later experience our identity as universal consciousness.

At the beginning, the personality that we perceive ourselves as being is emblematic of the ego because it conforms to a low level of spiritual evolution and operates mostly identified with the physical body and by following external conditions without the knowledge of the soul.

After you detect the soul's illumination, you can proceed to recognize it as your real identity, which is the main purpose of the self-realization of the personality. The soul is your genuine identity, which doesn't come from your physical, emotional, ethereal, or mental bodies.

Stage 2: The Self-Realization of Individuality

The second stage of spiritual development is the self-realization of individuality. It begins when you sense your vital energy flowing through the ethereal body. When you can detect this flow of energy, you begin the process of awakening the three centers of the soul.

As you advance through this process, your recognition of the soul becomes stronger. After having recognized both the illumination of the soul within the mental body—the flow of consciousness—and the flow of vital energy within your ethereal body, you are ready to begin your evolution into your soul—becoming a soul-embodied person.

The process of evolving into a soul-embodied person is the self-realization of individuality. During this stage of awakening, you awaken each of your three soul centers through the practice of surrendering.

Your connection with the soul during the initial stages of spiritual evolution is unsteady. You can easily lose contact with the soul because there is interference within your ethereal, emotional, and mental bodies. Our senses are used to operating within the external environment, so sense perceptions can distract us. For this reason, it is necessary to develop your senses to help you connect with your soul.

To transform the centers of the soul, the practice is to purify the energy flowing within our ethereal, emotional, and mental bodies.

In Stage 2, you begin by awakening the ethereal body. From the ethereal body, you gain access to and awaken the emotional body. From the emotional body, you gain access to and awaken the mental body. By awakening the ethereal, emotional, and mental bodies in turn, you establish the proper environment within yourself to blend your soul with your personality.

During this stage, you integrate the three purified soul centers to obtain the complete illumination of your physical existence by the soul. Here, you will graduate to a soul-infused personality because you are embodying the soul. This is a significant achievement during your spiritual evolution.

You can transform your personality into a higher self (or truer self) through the self-realization of individuality. After which, you function mainly by following the guidance from the soul.

The self-realization of individuality requires you to make a concerted effort throughout your lifespan. you need to make this goal your priority and follow through. Success in this endeavor involves real commitment, real dedication.

Many people find other goals more important than the goal of evolving into the soul and end up postponing its pursuit. Even so, it is the main purpose for our existence. And fortunately, there are twenty-four hours in the day, so we can hold a job, maintain families and relationships, and work on embodying our souls. These goals are not mutually exclusive.

Frankly, doing everything necessary to transform into the soul is not for the crowd. Only those who are willing to do what is necessary will succeed. But it is worth it. Those who do pursue this path ultimately find the soul-infused life tremendously peaceful, meaningful, and rewarding. Being guided by our souls adds new dimensions to who we are and what we are capable of perceiving and contributing.

Stage 3: The Self-Realization of Universality

The third stage of spiritual development is the self-realization of universality. In this stage, we transcend our individuality and merge with the source of creation and universal consciousness.

During this stage, you will start by merging with your soul! In meditation, you will begin registering your identity as only a soul without influence from your physical body. The awareness of the soul that you have experienced through your senses will relax and you will be liberated as a soul. At this juncture, you will be only your soul registering consciousness and without perceiving it with your physical body.

The self-realization of universality has two complementary stages. One stage is registering exclusively as a soul when moving to join the universal consciousness while the body rests. The other stage is returning from this previous stage to infuse your personality (the aspect of you that functions with a body) with the light of universal consciousness.

Initially, you will experience the soul as awareness within the mental body. But then, when you surrender your sense of awareness, you will liberate the soul to merge with universal consciousness. At this moment, you will be "only your soul" without experiencing it through your body! You will be exclusively registering pure consciousness.

After the soul merges into the field of universal consciousness, it returns to establish a link with our physical ethereal, emotional, and mental bodies. At the end of the process, we are in unity with the soul and universal consciousness.

In Stage 3, you will experience a condition of wholeness that occurs after having integrated the personal, individual, and universal levels of your existence into one. You can consider the evolutionary process complete once you have realized your true self on these three levels of self-realization. By this point, you will have transformed your perception from a regular human point of view into a universal perspective.

During this stage, you become a soul-infused personality with a direct link to universal consciousness. We call it the self-realization of universality because this is the beginning of the soul's union and evolution into the universal source of creation. Liberated from the constraints of the human condition, the soul returns to fulfilling its evolutionary purpose: to express itself fully within the context of our human existence.

The Ego

We, as human beings, have the capacity for self-reflection. This cognitive ability differentiates us from other living beings. And it is this ability that creates the ego, which is our subjective personal interpretation, or sense, of our existence. For that reason, the term *ego* can express either a true or a false identity. Which one depends on our current reasoning; and more specifically, on the evolutionary stage of our individual consciousness.

In its most basic form, the ego introduces us to reality from a physical and relative point of view. When we achieve a more advanced spiritual condition, the ego evokes reality from a universal point of view as an expression of the soul.

Problems arise when we let our egos interpret our reality only through the most basic form. It is common to find people experiencing their egos as their real identity. When this happens, the ego continues to reflect our ignorance and blocks our spiritual evolution.

The ego's real function—beyond keeping the body alive—is to retrieve information from the soul. The support of the ego is very important to our physical, emotional, and mental bodies; however, we also need to continuously surrender it so that we can access our true identity.

When I use the word *surrender*, I mean relinquishing the view of reality only based on a relative world. We need to give up on the desires that those views create along with the actions that those desires generate. Refer to Chapter 10, "Stabilization of the Mental Body," for a detailed explanation of this concept.

The ego, which is a form of mental activity, claims to be the master of the physical dimension and it will always try doing anything to remain. It is only after we recognize the nature and purpose of the ego that we stop being just egos and start connecting to our soul.

Even though the main purpose of our existence within the physical dimension is transcending our minds and personalities, none of us will ever be able to fully surrender our ego prior to our self-realization of universality. Ego is an inherent part of the human existence. It naturally remains with us during every stage of our spiritual evolution because it is a purely mental construct and a byproduct of our relative intelligence. Without an ego, we would not be able to witness our inner awakening states or support our self-realization.

Since ego is present through the self-realization process, we need to be very careful about sidestepping its deceitful advice. For instance, during the initial levels of our inner state exploration, the ego tries to persuade us to stop and begin focusing on something else. As ego gradually surrenders its dominance to the soul during the awakening process, it may begin claiming the wisdom of the soul throughout each of the levels of our self-development. Even after our soul has reached an advanced state of purification and healing, the ego will persist in showing up and trying to dominate our thinking. The ego is so tricky that it can make us believe that we have come to this world with a unique purpose to play out or make us assume that someone has chosen us for a special mission.

The reality is that the ego will always show up trying to assert its supremacy without fundament. Only our spiritual evolution can defeat its continuous attempts to provide us with an identity that defines us in a limited role. Our true selves have unlimited potential.

As difficult as it seems, the reality is that, in the end, ego does not have the capacity to obstruct our spiritual path.

During self-realization, as we evolve and experience ever more refined inner states, the ego begins to surrender to the soul. Then, it transforms and begins helping to advance our evolution. It begins serving the purpose of embodying the soul and we start perceiving it as being more tranquil and understandable.

Prior to the final stage of self-realization as a universal being, the ego will still be present. We will have to continue surrendering it until the final day of our existence within the physical dimension and die.

In summary, our spiritual goal, therefore, is not to eliminate the ego but instead to transform it to serve the purpose of our spiritual evolution.

Chapter 5

THE MYSTERY OF SOLITUDE

We may experience solitude before, as well as during, all the phases of our awakening process. It is an inseparable companion of the spiritual path.

We can experience solitude from both a situational and an emotional point of view. Situational solitude refers to our location and circumstances, whereas emotional solitude relates to the sensations we experience during an event. We could be surrounded by people and feel just as alone as we do when we're physically isolated.

While the word *solitude* sometimes has the connotation of being an unpleasant emotional response to isolation, we also need to recognize that we can be alone without experiencing any bad sensation from it. It is our belief system that classifies the solitude condition and immediately provides an emotional reaction to it.

Some people fear being alone because they do not want to experience any painful sensation from it. This happens to us if we were raised to look for support from others. When we realize that they are not there for us, a bad perception of loneliness begins.

The truth is that we should neither be frightened of situational solitude nor the emotional responses it may cause. What most of us do not know, is that there is a powerful, dormant force beyond the experience of solitude that can benefit us. In due time, we may gradually come to recognize that the loneliness we go through has a special purpose and can help us in numerous ways. It provides us with the opportunity to explore our inner dimensions. It assists us in ending our overidentification with the external world. It creates an adequate environment in which to discover our true selves.

When we spend time in solitude, we may begin to feel lonely. We may miss the company of our family or other people close to us because we are accustomed to their presence. We may also feel isolated, anxious, and frustrated by not getting the company that we want.

During this period, it may be hard for us to understand that feeling incomplete without the presence of others is an erroneous perception. It may sound counterintuitive, but when we feel bad during solitude it is because we are not connected with our true selves, not because we are missing something or someone out there.

The best way to deal with painful loneliness is by letting it arise in you and going through it without any resistance. We need to let go of our attachment to whatever thoughts and emotional triggers are causing it and turn our attention inward to look for our real self. As we enter deeper connection with our real selves, we alleviate our sense of loneliness.

During the awakening period, we progressively experience relief from the bad sensations of loneliness; however, we will encounter a different discomfort throughout this process because we begin transforming and adjusting into our real selves.

The uncomfortable sensations experienced during the awakening period won't be the same for everybody because we all have diverse life experiences. We come to the process of spiritual exploration with different spiritual conditions than others, therefore the progress we make will be distinct. One individual will have more or fewer attachments to relinquish than another. Surrendering will be different for everyone.

The most likely reality is that an uncomfortably arduous sensation, along with a transformation of personality, happens to those who are going through the process of awakening their souls.

The process of linking to the true self begins with a painful dropping of previous conceptual schemes of identity and relationship with those around us. In general, it leads to changes in our belief systems.

During the process of recognizing our true selves, we change our perceptions about the external world and, as a result, the structure of the ego begins to collapse. Throughout this transformation, the social structure around us that represents our reality—our friends, family, job, profession, activities, belongings, and so on—and which has been continuously resonating with our ego, begins shifting so we experience a new reality. During our personal transformation, our alignment with others, particularly with friends and family members, must adjust. As our priorities change, some activities will seem less important to us than they once did. Shifting our condition impacts our social relationships if we no longer connect others through the milieu of shared values.

Changes of personality may raise concerns for our family and friends. Some people will accept the transformation, but others will entirely reject us because of it. People close to us are normally more impacted than casual acquaintances and their responses can be absolutely negative as they begin worrying what could be happening to us. It is common to experience some extreme reactions from family members during awakening as they mistakenly believe that we are completely unhappy or mad about life—or imagine that we are rejecting them. They may think we're mentally disordered. It may be difficult for them to understand that we are undergoing a remarkable transformation that is beneficial to us.

For our own part, our sense of the ego and how we perceive reality completely changes. It can feel like a kind of death to transform our personality while finding a real identity and reconnecting to the soul.

It is impressive to see how loneliness begins to dissipate and any need for distraction spontaneously drops off once we are connecting deeply with the true self—the soul. The call for amusement while engaging socially with people around us progressively dissolves and we begin appreciating being with our soul in solitude.

Gradually, our relationships with others and the world around us start to change. When we spend time with our friends and loved ones, our experience becomes more relaxed and freer from dependence. We no longer have to go through perplexing attempts to get someone to fill a missing space in us. This happens because our sense of aloneness gradually is replaced by a sense of oneness. We do not need to look outside for fulfillment because we are complete when we embody the presence of the soul.

This is how we begin to appreciate spending time with our soul and it becomes our best friend. Then, anytime we are alone, we do not experience bad sensations and a continuously blissful peace arrives.

Many spiritual practitioners fail to follow the path of the soul because they feel uncomfortable or even scared about the prospect of being alone. It is incredible how many people run away the moment they think about being alone, mostly because they aren't ready to let go of something they have.

People are often comfortable within traditional groups that follow false and imaginary spiritual goals, most likely because they can continue functioning from the perspective of their ego. It may be hard for them to understand that the quest for the soul is an exploration of their individual inner self and not an exploration of the crowd's mentality.

Be prepared for solitude because it is a condition of our spiritual evolution. At a certain point in our lives, aloneness would help us establish a connection to our soul. When this time comes, we have the option to surrender or continue resisting it. We can always try it now. But we can also wait until later, or even for a different life! No matter what, remember that the one who suffers the pain of loneliness is the ego. It suffers because it completely identifies with the external world and is not connected to the soul.

This may be the time to begin the real work so do not be afraid about solitude because it will help you in the process of awakening your soul.

PART TWO

THE SELF-REALIZATION OF PERSONALITY

Chapter 6

BEYOND PERSONALITY

Self-realization of personality is a concept that people define in different ways. Commonly, it is viewed as satisfying the full range of our needs, reaching our full potential, and contributing to the good of humankind and society.

While all these descriptions seem reasonable, they refer solely to psychological realization. In general, they imply that our goal is to become an ideal or perfect person. Most definitions of self-realization of personality only consider the physical, emotional, and mental aspects of being human—in the psychological portions of human nature. Most do not consider the spiritual dimension of our nature. To be clear, the word *spiritual* relates to more than our "religious needs."

In actuality, self-realization of personality is a complex experience. It surpasses the top boundary of psychological content and is more than cultivating an educated personality or expressing good ethical principles.

Most religions provide their believers with a set of moral rules to follow in the name of goodness and for the sake of self-improvement and salvation. Some traditional followers misunderstand evolution and think that they must learn codes of conduct, polish their behaviors, and, in some cases, become saints. They follow norms of conduct that only keep followers occupied, which ultimately produce culpability and denial. They act in erroneous ways because of assuming that the spiritual path is about the improvement of the psychological self.

We should not confuse perfection with purification and healing. Self-realization is something special that always takes us beyond our personality. Realization is not about becoming impeccable at a human level in order to attain salvation. It is about learning how to maintain psychological equilibrium to purify and heal the human condition so our emotions and thoughts no longer drive us away from the soul.

Everyone knows that life is temporary. But some don't realize that the life they're leading is just a stage in a more expansive existence, and that each of us is born for the main purpose of learning how to transcend the human condition—not to spend our whole life refining it.

The truth is that a self-realized being attains most characteristics of an ideal human being without following codes of conduct because of inspiration that comes from the soul. This individual's behavior emanates from within. Conduct that comes from rules is like ornamental fruit hung on an artificial Christmas tree, whereas soul-inspired conduct is similar to the real fruit that comes from a living tree.

We will never be able to find peace, much less freedom, by educating ourselves and trying to refine our personality because, by nature, the personality is imperfect and in pain.

The purpose for the process of self-realization is not to benefit the personality. Rather, it is to become disciplined and habituated enough to express the soul's purpose. Self-realization is, therefore, an accomplishment of the soul. We are not here to refine our personality; we are here to transcend it!

The Purpose of Self-Realization of Personality

The main purpose for the self-realization of personality is to recognize our identity as a soul, which doesn't originate from our physical, emotional, or mental bodies.

The self-realization of personality is a very subtle process through which we perceive our true identity without any psychological relationship or reference to our human nature. When we recognize the presence of the soul, we understand the true nature of our identity and are able to correctly answer the fundamental question, "Who am I?"

Until we link to our soul, each of us lives as a regular human being with a "borrowed" identity—one that is shaped by our encounters with the external, physical world and hand-me-down beliefs and behaviors.

To recognize the true self is a process of awakening awareness by creating synergy between the soul and the mental body. During this process, we are establishing a bridge of communication between the ego and the soul. We are detecting consciousness—the energy of the soul—mirrored in the mental body.

The majority of people on Earth at any given time are somewhere in the midst of the process of discovering their true identities as souls. Some may have a natural sense of awareness of their souls at birth while some others claim to have awakened their souls by interacting with the energy of an advanced spiritual practitioner.

The awakening of awareness has two basic stages. The first is the stage of becoming a self-aware observer. The second is the stage of turning into a conscious observer to then experience awareness (the illumination of the soul)

In the next chapter, we will explore the process in detail.

Chapter 7

BECOMING A SELF-AWARE OBSERVER

One of the most important concepts before starting the process of awakening awareness is understanding how we, as ordinary observers, perceive the world around us. There is no definitive way to perceive the world, as how everyone perceives depends on their individual perspective, which is based both upon their current situation and their relative point of view.

The human mind forms an impression of reality based on relationships and comparisons. For example, when we have a new experience, we immediately compare it with something that we've previously experienced. And it is only after finding a point of reference, like recalling a prior event or psychological state, that our new experience has a meaning to us.

When you are a regular observer, your relationship to the external world is the basis of your identity. This is normal. And it means the observer is the same as the ego.

Under most circumstances, you only use the exterior world as a reference to locate yourself. Every time you refer to something in the external world as a means of defining your identity, you create separation—not union--between you and your point of reference.

The dimension in which we live is always a relative dimension because it depends on temporary relationships. Everything that exists in space and time is constantly changing. Even the observer is temporary because space and time change each of us. We age. We die. Our bodies disintegrate and feed the plants. The plants grow and feed us. Relative reality is the narrow lens through which regular observers see. To them, there is nothing else beyond their circumstances.

For most people, this might sound totally normal but the reality is different.

The most interesting and deepest, spiritual evolution of the human being occurs in dimensions beyond the physical. This assertion will only seem valid when the regular observer evolves and discovers their real identity (the soul).

Identifying with your soul does not mean that you will begin living without the relationships you've formed in space and time—because, obviously, you are not only a soul. No matter how awakened you become, you will still continue to be a human being bound by the physical laws of the universe until the day your body dies. But the soulful aspect of your being is an extension of your soul.

Ideally, you will cultivate a balance between these two dimensions of your being. You will potentially, one day, recognize yourself as a soul living in the physical world.

Humankind is at the edge of evolution into our spiritual dimension. What will this be like for you? When you develop your observational skills, the ignorant and relative condition of the animal kingdom will stay behind and you will awaken your awareness. You will be able to recognize your soul as your real identity. This moment will commence your advanced evolution into pure consciousness.

So, let us see how we begin evolving from regular observers to observers at the next immediate level--the level of self-awareness—a shift of perception that is the very first step in recognizing our real identities as souls.

As infants, we become aware of our existence as individuals by differentiating ourselves from our external environment, including the people around us.

The people whom I am calling *regular observers* are such because they are cognitively immersed in the belief systems of the collective mind. To create a sense of self, aka a personality or self-definition, they operate in a largely subconscious manner while directing their attention towards the external world. This is where they look to define the meaning of their existence. On an internal, subjective level, because of being overidentified with their surroundings, their identity is superficial and transitory. To themselves, they appear to exist exclusively as physical beings.

Of course, a person's identity as a human being is only valid while that person is alive in the physical dimension. Any identity created within this context will naturally be somewhat associated with the body. But also, by their personality when the definition has a purely psychological content. A personality is developed in the context of physical, emotional, and mental influences.

In time, when our bodies die, our identification with them will vanish even though our identities as souls will persist. The identity as a human is a temporary identity and not our original one.

Our original identities are eternal because these are located beyond psychological structures and belong to our souls. As humans, we may not see the soul because it is in a different "place." The person and the soul reside in different dimensions. However, the person is an extension of the soul.

We like to imagine that our souls are connected to us all the time, but in reality, our souls are not connected to us until we can truly experience their presence. The meditation practices I am espousing to you in this book are designed to facilitate the experience of soul connection, first and foremost.

Why might we be disconnected from our souls? The mental body can become congested with thoughts and ideas about our world. These easily distort how we approach our inner condition, preventing us from discovering the soul.

This is why it is better, when trying to access our real identity, to do it without the influence of factors that originated within the confines of our personality. Accessing the soul for the first time is only possible if we enter our mental body and clear away distracting external factors. And this is made possible by practicing meditation.

During meditation practice, we need to proceed with mental relaxation instead of concentration. When are practicing concentration, we associate and fix experiences into our mind, whereas when we are practicing relaxation, we isolate ourselves and disconnect from external influences.

Our aim is to quiet the mind, the initial step of meditation. Mental relaxation helps us dissipate our thoughts and, in general, cease mental activity.

If we want to recognize the existence of our soul, we need to go beyond the simple act of asking, "Who am I?" We need to observe the energy of the mental body and try to identify the one who is making observations. Become aware of that presence. This is a critical step in exploring our real identity.

Initially, as we are seeking the observer within us, we may encounter different aspects of the ego: our impulses, thoughts, and memories of experiences that formed our personal identity in the physical dimension. As we relax the mental body and continue seeking the observer, all these aspects will begin to disappear.

By turning our attention to our mental body and looking for the observer, we are diverting our attention away from external events and inward towards those happening within our own selves.

We need to be careful here: The intention during this phase of meditation is not either to neglect the external world or to deny the existence of the body. Keep in mind that you cannot neglect the body or the physical dimension! There has to be someone practicing meditation, otherwise who is doing it?

It is when we enter our inner energetic dimension and place our attention upon the energy of the mental body that we become *self-aware observers*. Our self-defined identities progress from the condition of regular observation to the condition of self-observation or self-contemplation. We are doing more than observing our thoughts.

During this phase, a self-aware observer is using self-referencing to analyze the energy of the mental body albeit still without realizing the existence of the true self. So far, this is a phase of crude energetic mental observation!

Self-reference allows the ego—a personality construct associated with the body and emotions—to refer back to itself! This process is similar to the moment of self-observation in which the ego is acknowledging its existence. This recognition is established within the constraints of the mind where the ego is observing itself.

Chapter 8

BECOMING A CONSCIOUS OBSERVER

As our evolution continues, we become self-aware observers and able to relax more and focus our attention deeper into our internal energetic field. During meditation, our internal attention becomes more constant while our external reference points gradually disappear.

When a self-aware observer begins sensing the absence of recognition of external events, there is a bizarre sense of nonidentification. The self-observer starts experiencing his or her identification in a dull form.

This dullness is a strange perception since we normally draw our identity from a correlation with external experiences. Any time perceptions of familiar experiences are not present, we become incapable of forming a clear identity. The absence of an externally generated self-image gives us an abstract sense of our identity, a muted subjectivity.

This perception is the sense of the self-aware observer knowing itself as a subject within a quiet mind. And it is an experience that makes us feel suffocated.

BECOMING A CONSCIOUS OBSERVER

As the self-aware observer continuous relaxing and abiding in its primary subjectivity, the energy of the mental body declines. The observer's self-awareness expands, letting the observer perceive a source of identity illuminating its mind.

It is when our self-aware observer deeply relaxes and self-referencing ceases that a deeper transformation begins. Within this new condition, the self-aware observer surpasses the stage of just being aware of itself and becomes aware of the illumination of the soul.

When we reach this phase in our cognitive evolution, we transition from self-awareness into awareness. We become aware of the energy of the soul whose consciousness is being emulated by our mental body. This is how we originally can realize the real source of our identity.

The presence of the soul in us transforms the dull subjectivity of the self-aware observer into a meaningful sensation of illumination. The self-aware observer becomes a *conscious observer* due to the energy emanating from the soul. Much more than discovering our true identity, we also begin the process of evolving and transforming into it. Embodying it. We begin discarding the externally generated image of our self and allowing an authentic image to emerge.

With the illumination of the soul, the conscious observer stops using external factors to produce a false identity. The observer begins to know itself as a subject that exists behind the mind. The presence of the soul allows the conscious observer to have a meaning beyond thoughts and objects.

At this stage of awakening, we have the capacity to sense the meaning our existence without any personal or psychological content. We can sense our "self" with the presence of the soul as an impersonal experience.

As a conscious observer, we realize that we are an essence and not a form. We understand that our physical bodies are only transient elements of our existence.

We may continue interacting with others as people regularly do in the physical dimension; however, we also recognize that our legitimate identity is not the one generated during this physical phase of our existence.

The Awakening of Awareness

The subtle sensation of mental awareness is just a reflection of the soul's consciousness—energy emanated by the soul.

As we gradually begin transcending the fluctuations of our thoughts, we have a sensation of clarity. This expands, filling our mental body and letting us experience our soul's existence.

We are able to understand who we are within a quiet mind. During the awakening of awareness, we are only making initial contact with our soul. We are sensing the glow of the soul emulated into our mental body. But there is a sense of presence.

With the presence of the soul, we begin meditation. Without the presence of the soul, it is only relaxation. Strengthening the presence of the soul is our main goal during the next following practices.

We need to consider the awakening of awareness as a weak experience of the soul because the mental body is still under the heavy influence of both ethereal and emotional energy, which is largely uncontrolled. During this stage, we are only experiencing a small flash of the soul's presence; nevertheless, this is the spark that will guide us through the evolutionary process of transforming into our soul.

PART THREE

THE SELF-REALIZATION OF INDIVIDUALITY

Chapter 9

THE QUEST FOR THE SOUL

The self-realization of individuality is a significant step that takes us squarely into the spiritual kingdom. For me, this signifies the moment in which we genuinely enter the practice of spirituality.

Before advancing into this section, I would like to offer you a word of caution. The path that leads to the self-realization of individuality is much narrower than the path of the self-realization of personality. If you decide to continue the journey of the self-realization of individuality, I promise you that everything in your life will change dramatically. In fact, your life as you currently are living it is in a huge peril if you decide to continue.

Consider yourself forewarned! If you do not feel comfortable about change, please stop. It is not that you will be hurt or die if you go this route or if you are unable to meet the challenge. But what you may lose during the self-realization of individuality could seem to you (at least in the short-term) a more significant loss than the loss of your physical existence.

If you decide to continue the path of self-realization of individuality, you will enter a challenging stage beyond awakening when your ethereal, emotional, and mental bodies are undergoing purification. During this stage, you will be on route to embodying the soul and experiencing the reality of life, which is to conquer eternity. You won't be in the darkness any longer because you will have transcended the lower dimensions of existence to join the Beloved (universal source), which will illuminate you.

During this stage of your self-realization, your physical body will still be alive but you could feel as if you have died, and afterwards you will be completely new. You will emerge with a new and different identity and consciousness because you will become a purified self.

The self-realization of individuality is not meant for a person who only wants to explore a frontier or know something else, because curiosity is not enough for someone to experience the soul. This path is for people who are ready, those who have evolved enough to embody their souls.

Furthermore, there is no shame in moving forward slowly. Each of us needs to become spiritually mature for the soul to enter our existence. If you currently feel unready to continue the journey, I suggest revisiting the chapter on the self-realization of personality and waiting. Do the meditations. Allow yourself a chance to evolve at your own pace. Perhaps sometime later you will recognize the presence of your soul and realize that it is now the right time to be ambitious about your spiritual endeavors.

Always remember that the main purpose of our existence in the physical dimension is our evolution into the soul. Our real purpose is not to become a perfect human being but to transcend the physical dimension of existence.

If you are able to appreciate the duality between the identity of your ego and the identity of "I am," then you are ready! You have the engine needed to propel yourself forward on this path. By recognizing your real identity, you have the energy required to evolve into your soul.

Let me briefly explain. The self-realization of individuality is the process of integrating your individuality with the three centers of "I am": the ethereal, emotional, and mental bodies. The main characteristic of self-realization of individuality is the transformation of the ego to have unity with the soul.

It is through the awakening of the ethereal, emotional, and mental bodies that we gradually transform into a pure self. Surrendering to the presence of "I am" facilitates the purification and healing processes. Once the ego fully surrenders to the soul, it becomes a pure self illuminated by the presence of the soul.

The transformation into a pure self is a result of mastering the energy of the ethereal, emotional, and the mental bodies. When we complete the self-realization of individuality, the pure self and soul blend into one and start functioning as a whole. They no longer act separately. As an embodied soul, we will naturally follow the laws of the universal source (which I prefer to call the Beloved).

The self-realization of individuality involves two major tasks: awakening the ethereal body and awakening the emotional body. Later, these activities will contribute to the transformation and stabilization of the mental body. The final step in the process of self-realization of individuality is the integration or unification of the three centers of the soul.

Chapter 10

STABILIZATION OF THE MENTAL BODY

As we discussed at the end of the last chapter, two key parts in the self-realization of individuality are the purification and the mastering of the mental body. The stabilization of the mental body is a long process that is essential for our spiritual evolution. To accomplish this objective, we must continue striving to purify our mental body and exercise constant recognition of our soul's presence.

During this chapter, I want to introduce some concepts that are necessary to understand the process of stabilization of the mental body. Here, I am only defining the concepts without giving details of their development, which will be explained in later chapters. At the beginning, stabilization may appear complex; however, as you advance through the book, you should gain a better understanding of the whole process.

Two essential practices lead us to stabilize our mental body and contribute, in general, to our self-realization. The first practice is self-remembrance. The second is the surrendering of energy from the ethereal and emotional bodies.

During the stabilization of the mental body, we transform the ego into a pure self at the awareness level so that we can arrive at a condition of mental transparency. Throughout the transformation, we gradually embody the soul. Embodiment is an intricate process that requires the purification of both the ethereal and emotional bodies. Because of their interconnection with the mental body and one another they have direct influence over it.

The mental body, which serves as a control center for our ethereal and emotional bodies, is powered by the energy of the soul. Since we discovered our link with the soul during the self-realization of our personality, our work during this stage is to keep this connection alive. Fortunately, we can preserve the link between the soul and the mental body through the practice of self-remembrance. But we should not forget that the practice of self-remembrance alone is insufficient to maintain the link.

Considering that the mental body is equally affected by the ethereal and emotional bodies, our connection with the soul can become unstable. Instability is caused by emotional and ethereal energies flowing among the three centers of the soul. If we want to maintain our connection with the soul, we therefore have to be cautious about anything in any of these centers that is affecting our mental body.

The good news is that we can control these energies and reduce their impact on us through the process of surrendering.

To reiterate, if we want to keep the connection with our soul, we need to stabilize the energy of our mental body. This is possible by practicing both self-remembrance and surrender.

Self-Remembrance and Presence

Self-remembrance is the continuous effort to maintain the presence of the soul (your real identity). The objective is to keep an unbroken sense of awareness or pure consciousness reflected in your mind.

Here, I refer to *reflection* because your mental body is emulating the energy coming from the soul (consciousness) as a sense of awareness. In other words, the light that emanates from the soul is expressed in the mental body.

If you already have gone through the process of self-realization of personality, then the process of remembering your real identity may be much easier for you, particularly during your meditation sessions. However, even if you want to recognize your real identity at all times, you cannot spend the whole day practicing meditation. Therefore, recognizing your identity when you are not meditating is the next challenge to meet. This is an entirely different situation.

To remember your real identity not only during meditation but also in the midst of your daily activities, you will need to practice self-remembrance.

During the early stages of the awakening of awareness, we can recognize our real identity, but this recognition is not strong and it is discontinuous. We will experience pure subjectivity and be able to identify the presence of the soul only for short periods of time.

This happens because the link we have to the soul is still weak. Additional work must be done to fortify this connection. We need to consolidate that condition to the point that it becomes natural during all our daily activities.

Eventually, the recognition of our "real identity" will become continuous and we will be able to sense the link without any effort throughout all our activities.

When deliberately practicing self-remembrance during daily activities, you may find that you begin by remembering your real identity for a few seconds and then forgetting about it. After a few minutes or hours, you realize you forgot and you try again, but you still keep on forgetting. Don't get frustrated if this happens, because the more frequently you attempt to remember your soul's presence the longer the periods of its presence will last.

There's no race to the finish line. You can forget many times but as long as you start again, sooner or later your forgetfulness habit will stop. Then you will experience unbroken continuity of the presence of your soul.

The practice of self-remembrance begins by transforming your mind. Through it, you will return to your original nature. Your mind begins emulating your real and eternal identity. During advanced levels of self-realization, you will be able to distinguish your ego from your soul like you can distinguish any other objects around you from one another. You, as your soul, will take the control and you will be capable of seeing how your ego acts as if you are located a few inches behind the back of your head.

You can compare the experience to the one of driving a car, when you can see the surroundings of the cabin from your seat and hear the noise of the engine. This sound helps you perceive how the engine responds when you press or ease up on the gas pedal. Because you are in control of this action, you can detect if there is something going wrong with the car.

It is important to understand that your soul is not only connected to your mind and body like a driver in a car. The soul is so intimately associated with the mind that it as if it were intermixed with it. They are unified because they are both dimensions of your being; however, there is also a certain duality between them.

During the self-realization of personality, the mind becomes aware of the presence of the soul. When the soul is present, you can sense the participation of two parts of you: The mind represents your so-called ego and the soul represents your so-called higher self. You will continue to experience yourself as having a dual personality throughout your awakening process until you accept the soul as your real identity.

Prior to the awakening of awareness, the ego is entirely self-referencing. But once the ego awakens and you are experiencing duality between the mind and the soul, the ego recognizes the power of the soul through the illumination of the mental body. Next, as soon as the ego is able to recognize itself as the mind in separation from the soul, you are ready to start practicing self-remembrance. That's the signal of your readiness for this step in the sequence of your meditations.

When you are capable of observing your ego, your identification with it will never come back again. You will continue to use it for social convenience and to conduct all normal daily activities you undertake in the physical dimension. But as you progress, your ego will begin relaxing and helping you succeed in your evolution into your soul.

If you want to get the results described above, you need to practice self-remembrance along with the act of surrendering. The practice of self-remembrance alone will not contribute to the self-realization of individuality. I will offer specific details about this within the following chapter on the self-realization of individuality.

The awakening of awareness is an extremely important event in the journey of our spiritual path; however, the image of the soul we perceive in the mind is only a pale imitation of the energy of the soul, like a reflection in a mirror that's hanging in a dimly lit hallway. When you awaken awareness, you will have a spontaneous realization of your real identity; however, the presence of the soul is not yet permanent.

The constant refocusing of your attention during self-remembrance enables you to go beyond your default mode of self-referencing. Some people find it difficult to distinguish between self-referencing and self-remembering. The only way I know of to truly make the distinction is to continuously look for the presence of the soul. This is how to transcend the duality of the ego and the soul. The moment that you stop identifying with the soul you get lost and become overly identified with the external world. That's self-reference.

Until you finally establish permanent identification with your soul while you're doing all our activities your attention will continue to alternate between the soul and the ego. It is important for the ego to be purified. The pure self that we transform to is the one that actually practices self-remembrance.

As I said previously, through the practice of self-remembrance, we stabilize the mental body and begin to sustain our contact with the soul. We are sensing the presence of the soul as its essence is reflected in the mind.

We can experience self-remembrance only within the purified mental body, not within the heart or another part of the body. Through the mind, the self acknowledges its identity as the soul.

Initially, the recognition of this true identity will only be a sudden impulse in your conscious awareness. But as you practice self-remembrance, your glimpses of recognition and your perceptual shift of identification will last longer, until one day the understanding that your soul is your identity becomes a natural condition in your life.

Practicing self-remembrance during the run-of-the-mill activities of everyday life, not only during meditation, will provide you with an increasingly strong ability to retain the perception of "I am" that is characteristic of the soul.

Experiencing awareness without experiencing a sense of "I am" is not true self-remembrance. Self-remembrance requires there to be teamwork between the ego of an individual whose mental body is being purified and the soul.

Self-remembrance is not an exercise in which we fall into a trance and lose track of who we are, as some individuals do in an effort to alleviate their suffering. When practicing self-remembrance, our real identity is always present and we are always conscious because the soul is constantly illuminating the mind.

Self-remembrance also is not a single phase of inner work; it is a continuous practice undertaken during each and every phase of self-realization.

Surrendering

When I instruct you to *surrender*, the first thing I would like you to do is to stop fighting!

Within a spiritual context, when we surrender, we stop resisting the natural flow of things. We cease the resistance we are feeling toward ideas, outcomes, and emotions; in general, we give up on having control over anything. But most importantly, we surrender by following our own convictions, not because we lack options. We surrender because we completely accept and trust that everything will go well even without our input.

The firm confidence we have (or which our souls have) allows us to cease our resistance.

Trust is the main characteristic that arises during the process of surrender. We initially need to recognize the soul as our identity because it is the engine of the surrender process. As we progress in recognizing and trusting our soul, we then are willing to yield our control to its guidance.

As I mentioned before, the ego behaves as the expert of the physical dimension. So, if we decide to practice surrender, it is important to understand the characteristics of the ego because it will do anything to survive and retain its own tendencies.

During surrender, we relinquish the influence of the ego and its habits. We primarily surrender the view of reality based on a relative world. We surrender the desires that those views create along with the actions that those desires generate. Surrender occurs when the ego relaxes, letting the soul take the control—but as long as the ego shows up, the process of surrendering needs to continue.

The process of surrendering is neither developed nor controlled by the mind. In fact, the mind has to relax to facilitate the process. The ego must yield to the soul. When surrendering, we experience a wonderful, positive feeling of relaxation—of an end to effort, of relief. With the simple act of letting go, we are advancing from all our limitations and expanding into infinite possibilities.

The easiest way to surrender is during the practice of meditation, a time when you can quiet your mind and access the energy fields of the three centers of the soul. From there, you can surrender by administering the flow of energy within each center. The process is similar to the act of modifying software on a computer to get more optimal results. You stop the computer's activity, then go directly to the code and modify it to improve the outcome of a program. After that, you may restart the computer and continue running your program and you usually notice the device runs faster and easier.

During meditation, you need to relax your mental body to access your energetic field. You are using your brain, nervous system, and the organs of your body to initially detect the existing flow of energy within your ethereal, emotional, and mental bodies.

Having access to your inner energy is extremely important during the process of surrendering. You are going directly into the energy of your feelings, emotions, and thoughts.

Surrendering is a means of regulating the flow of energy in our ethereal and emotional bodies. When we become good at this, we have mastery of the process. This is how we become energetically transparent, transforming into a pure self so that our soul can illuminate our existence.

Surrendering is one of the most important practices of the spiritual path because it allows us to experience self-purification, which prepares us to return to the source of creation. Letting go of the ego during meditation is accomplished by displacing the ethereal, emotional, and mental energy in our inner field. This is the devoted act of the ego relinquishing its existence to the sacred and real essence, the soul.

The cause of surrendering is advanced through the purification of the three centers of the soul. You begin by surrendering the energy of the ethereal body, followed by surrendering the energy of the emotional body, and then, finally, the energy of the mental body. As you surrender, you are essentially giving up your whole life to the purpose of embodying your soul and merging with the absolute.

Of course, this doesn't mean that you will be abandoning the use of your physical body and its senses or being prevented from actively participating in the practicalities of your everyday life. You may even enjoy your senses, relationships, and work more than you did previously. Because you are less attached to certain outcomes, you will be able to accept people to be as they are—

even if they're not doing the same things as you or they disagree with your spiritual approach to life.

Life is a great teacher. Surrender anything and everything that disrupts your equanimity. Surrender anything in you that hints of ego.

Ultimately, most practitioners find that it is healthiest to strike a balance between surrendering and engagement with life.

The mental body is an energetic field that exchanges energy with the ethereal and emotional bodies and the exterior world. The flow of energy from these bodies normally produces impulses that originate thoughts and sensations in our minds. For this reason, to stabilize the mental body, we need to regulate the energy coming from our ethereal and emotional bodies.

Do not consider surrendering as a passive activity of waiting for something to happen by itself. Surrendering requires a combined effort from both the soul and the ego. It takes the commitment of the ego to allow the presence of the soul to be embodied.

By surrendering resistance and control over the flow of things, we expand the intimate relationship of the self and the soul. But really what's going on is the ego is stepping aside so the soul can replace it.

In surrendering to the soul, we are never surrendering to another person. It is our ego that surrenders. And it is not a single event; we need to continuously practice surrendering because the flow of energy into our body from the source of creation is constant.

If you want to experience a highly stable spiritual life, the act of surrendering should be an exercise you do in every moment of your existence no matter what else you are doing. Just run it like a program in the background. If you notice you're feeling some tension or having disrupted thoughts, pause and release. Let go.

In general, the process of surrendering begins by letting go of the ego to embody the soul and, later, advances to letting go of the soul to access the condition of absence.

We carry out the process of surrendering for two purposes. The first is to heal and or purify the ego so that we can embody our soul. The second is so that we may merge with the universal source of creation.

The deepest level of surrendering enables us to pass through the portal of absence. This is a condition in which we consciously enter the realm of the creation and are able to experience a state known as *samadhi of the absolute*, which I shall explain in detail in Chapter 15, "The Self-Realization of Universality."

The purification of the mental body occurs throughout the entire process of self-realization; however, it is during the self-realization of universality that we undertake the highest realization of consciousness.

Again, the description I have just given you is an extremely simplified summary. In this chapter, I am highlighting the importance of surrendering only because of how much it contributes to the stabilization of the mental body.

The Absolute

The concept of the *absolute* is known by different traditions and cultures of the world. The first time I heard about the absolute was in the context of Taoism, whose practitioners understand it as a condition of such purity that nothing exists yet and anything can be created.

This concept is very similar to the Zen Buddhist concepts of emptiness as *nonbeing* and presence as *being*.

Zen tradition defines the absolute as the inherent nature of everything and as a place of reality wherein all is created and to which all should ultimately return.

Some philosophical traditions consider the absolute the deepest dimension we can reach as human beings.

My understanding, as I have explained, is that entering the absolute requires the full surrender of the purified self to the soul through each of the centers of the soul—in other words, through the ethereal, emotional, and mental bodies in sequence. Each of the three soul centers provides us with a different qualitative experience of the absolute.

Accessing the absolute from a single dimension of our being means that we will have only a partial experience of the soul in that dimension. In general, however, access to the absolute is granted by fully surrendering energy from all three of the centers of the soul. Then, by crossing the gate simultaneously through all the three centers of the soul, we may experience full and unconditional union with absolute.

The Three Gates to the Absolute

The three gates through which we may enter the absolute exist in different dimensions. One of these portals is located in each of the ethereal, emotional, and mental bodies. When we go through any particular entrance, the absolute will seem to have different characteristics.

We may enter the absolute through the ethereal body by surrendering vital energy through the root chakra. We may enter the absolute through the emotional body by surrendering emotional energy through the solar plexus chakra. We may enter the absolute through the mental body by surrendering mental energy through the throat chakra.

These chakras act as boundaries or gates between existence and nonexistence within their respective bodies. We are able to traverse each of these gates by completely depleting the flow of energy in its corresponding dimension (ethereal, emotional, and mental).

It is important for us to learn how to sense the flow of energy moving through each center of the soul. Actually, being able to sense the flow of energy is different than assuming it is flowing. Sometimes meditation practitioners make the mistake of using their imaginations to establish a flow of energy; they do so by visualizing certain colors or thinking of certain sounds or vibrations. In both situations, they are only using their minds to fantasize. Our goal is simply to detect the flow.

We need to become sensitive enough to perceive energetic vibrations and flows that are already occurring instead of establishing them ourselves using mental force. Perception is made possible through the practice of surrendering.

Chapter 11

AWAKENING THE ETHEREAL BODY

The term *awakening of the ethereal body* is a reference to the activation of this inner, energetic field. The reason we would want to activate it is that we hope to integrate the energy of soul into this particular field.

During the awakening of awareness known as the self-realization of personality, we perceive the energy of the soul in our mind. This soul energy is what will guide us through the process of awakening the ethereal body.

The experience of awakening the ethereal body is different than the experience of awakening awareness. This distinction is important. During the awakening of awareness, we experience our real identity as a reflection of the soul's consciousness in our mental body.

By contrast, during the awakening of the ethereal body, we experience the essence of our existence, as a reflection of the soul illumination in our ethereal body.

The experience of awareness is an experience of the presence of the soul in the mind; but having this experience does not mean that we can suddenly sense the soul within our ethereal body too (or in the physical body, for that matter). It is only after awakening our ethereal body through surrendering its energy to the soul that we begin to sense the presence of the soul within this center. This new experience is the experience of "being."

Awakening your ethereal body will require you to purify its energy. Purity is one of the conditions that is necessary for you to experience the embodiment of your soul. Surrendering during meditation is the most effective exercise to purify the ethereal body.

The complete realization of the ethereal body occurs in two stages. First, purification. Second, merging with the absolute through the ethereal energy.

Surrendering Within the Ethereal Body

The process of surrendering ethereal energy is developed through the practice of meditation and by sending your attention directly into your inner energetic field. You have to access the raw ethereal energy flowing within your ethereal body and learn to control it.

Let us remember that the ethereal body center has three components: the root, spleen, and solar plexus chakras. Having energetic recognition of these chakras is very important if you want to access your ethereal energy. You need to be able to perceive the ethereal energy flowing through them before you can start surrendering it.

The flow of ethereal energy is most concentrated in the area of the spleen chakra, which lies in the middle of the ethereal body. This is the point in which we need to focus our attention at the beginning of this practice.

Like a door, the ethereal center of the soul can be activated in two directions. One direction the ethereal energy flows towards the ground—assuming you are seated in an upright position while you are meditating. The other direction ethereal energy flows towards the interior of the physical body. The door of energy exchange is located at the root chakra, at the bottom of the ethereal soul center. Vital energy in our case comes from the Earth and enters our bodies through the root chakra. When we surrender ethereal energy, it goes through the root chakra out of our bodies into the ground.

Within the ethereal soul center, the energy flows in two directions. Looking at it from an upright position, the flow goes down from the solar plexus chakra to the spleen chakra and them to the root chakra at the front side and inside the body. The flow goes up from the root chakra to the spleen chakra and them to the solar plexus chakra at the back side and inside of the body. The energy flow within the ethereal body is similar to a stream of water.

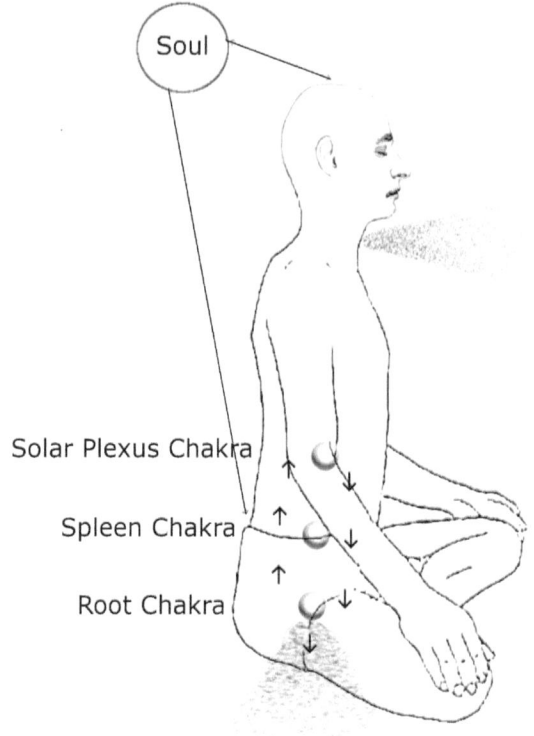

SURRENDERING ETHEREAL BODY ENERGY

The first step in the surrendering process is to recognize the flow of energy within your ethereal soul center.

Begin by sitting in meditation and calming the activity in your mind. Close your eyes and breathe naturally, letting yourself relax.

My advice to practice meditation is by adopting a seated position over a mat or pillow on the floor however you can do it by seating on a chair. Always meditate in a seated, upright position. You do not need to adopt a cross legged yoga position as shown in the figure above. The most important is that you feel comfortable on that position and that you be able to relax as a preliminary stage during meditation.

I will introduce three options to recognize the flow of energy within your ethereal body. Please chose the one that you find more comfortable.

Option 1

Begin by placing your attention in the middle of your lower abdomen. As you focus on this area, you may begin experiencing a warm sensation that progresses into a sense of heaviness. This is the sensation of ethereal energy.

Simply observe the flow, noticing if it is moving in any particular direction.

Focusing your attention on this area means you are lowering your mental awareness from the level of your head to your lower abdomen and maintaining it there.

Once you are able to detect the flow of energy within your abdomen, you are likely to notice more energy circulating there— one flow coming up from your root chakra and other coming from your solar plexus, but most moving through your spleen chakra.

Option 2

Your spleen chakra is located about three centimeters below your navel in the middle of your ethereal soul center. Your goal in this meditation is to sense energy flowing through it.

Begin seated, as in Option 1. Place the palm of one hand or one of your middle fingers below your navel.

A few seconds after you focus your attention in this area you will start sensing warmth. This progressively intensifies as energy transfers to the spleen chakra from your hand.

Maintain the posture for a few seconds, then place your hand in your lap.

The act of touching your belly is similar to lighting the wick of a candle with a match. In this case, the match is your hand or finger and the candle being ignited is your spleen chakra.

Continue focusing on the same area and you will sense the ethereal energy expanding throughout your abdomen.

After some practice you will begin sensing the energy of two streams one flowing up and other down through your spleen chakra.

Option 3

If the exercises above do not give you good results or you just want to spice up your meditation practice, you can use a crystal or metal singing bowl tuned to the natural vibrational frequency of the spleen chakra. Play it until you are able to sense the energy flowing into your lower abdomen. You can use the key of D, which vibrates at the frequency of the spleen chakra located in the middle of the ethereal soul center

***

After some practice, spending a few minutes per day with continuous focus on the lower abdomen during meditation, your ability to perceive ethereal energy will be heightened and the flow of energy within it be more evident.

When you are able to sense the energy flow within the ethereal body, you can begin the process of surrendering. At this point you can do a meditation in which you enter the ethereal body and merge with its flow.

Entering the ethereal body refers to the process of merging with the flow of your ethereal energy at the spleen chakra level and flowing down with it towards your root chakra and beyond. You are essentially becoming one with this energy while surrendering. Because one dimension of your being is ethereal, you are your own ethereal energy, therefore you are surrendering.

The process of surrendering is not a simple mental exercise related only to the action of displacing energy within your ethereal body. You also need to maintain an unbroken sense of awareness (the presence of the soul) throughout the surrendering practice as explained in "The Awakening of Awareness" and "Self-Remembrance" chapters (refer to pages 62 and 71 respectively).

During the initial part of the process, and with simple relaxation, we reduce the intensity of the ethereal energy flow; however, as you continue with the meditation practice you need to begin surrendering to direct and merge with the energy flow.

When you merge with the flow of energy, your ego is surrendering to the presence of the soul. In other words, your mental body is surrendering and it is also directing ethereal energy towards and through the root chakra.

As you continue meditating, the rate of the energy flow of your ethereal body will begin to ease and settle down to a slow rate. Advanced meditators will experience a subtle movement of ethereal energy from the top of their heads to the bottom of their torsos—the region of the root chakra. However, if you are just learning the practice of surrendering, it is more likely that you will sense the flow of your ethereal energy only near your spleen chakra.

No matter how long you've studied the art of surrendering, the best practice is this: As you enter into your ethereal energetic field, focus on the downflow of energy from the spleen chakra towards the root chakra and you will begin merging with it.

As you breathe, with each inhalation you maintain a sense of presence, and with each exhalation of relaxed breath, you continuously surrender your mind and dive from the middle of your ethereal soul center down into the depths of your root chakra. It is by letting go of thoughts and surrendering your existence that you begin resting and uniting with your soul.

This is how to begin letting go of the ethereal energy so you may in time experience the condition of being.

The Experience of Being

Being is a condition we experience when the energy of the ethereal body is flowing to the bottom of the torso during the process of surrendering.

The condition of being that you experience depends on the level of our spiritual awakening.

After you have completely purified the energy of your ethereal body through the process of surrender, you can call it the *pure self of being*.

Initially, ethereal energy is registered exclusively in the lower torso, within your ethereal soul center.

Then, as you evolve and your sensitivity is heightened, you can sense the stream of energy as being like a waterfall, starting in the head, then dropping into the chest, and ultimately moving down to the lower abdomen, where it exits the body through root chakra.

During the final stages of purification, the sensation of flowing ethereal energy disappears altogether and the ethereal body becomes transparent.

Before purification, you recognize flowing ethereal energy as a gentle warming and vibrating sensation that is making its way through each of the soul centers in turn. But really, you can only perceive this flow of energy passing through active, awakened centers. If you only have awakened the ethereal soul center, then you will only feel the experience of being in there.

The physical laws of the Earth influence the ethereal and physical components of your being. At the beginning, you perceive the heaviness of your ethereal energy being attracted by the gravity of the planet. The more that you surrender your energy, the less that you sense any such heaviness. This happens because when you surrender, you decrease the kinetic energy within the ethereal soul center.

During meditation, the condition of being starts with the surrender of your ethereal energy, which progresses until you embody the soul. At this point, you settle into an unconditional repose in the depth of the now.

The experience of being requires a continuous referencing of three aspects: identity, existence, and time. We acknowledge the identity aspect through the condition of presence and the illumination of the mental body by the light of the soul. You acknowledge the existence aspect through the condition of surrendering. And you acknowledge the time aspect by continuously leaving the immediate past and experiencing the now.

This whole process does not happen by itself with simple relaxation; it requires the practice of meditation. The experience of being is a continuous iteration of the soul, the mental body, and the ethereal body while surrendering. As I mentioned before, the mental body yields to the soul's presence and facilitates the purification of the ethereal energy through surrendering.

The ego within this process is represented by the portion of the mental body that acknowledges the existence of ethereal energy and the ethereal energy itself.

As the ego surrenders while directing ethereal energy out through the root chakra, the ethereal body begins to leave an empty space that at the same time fills up with the illumination of the soul. Meanwhile, the mental body is purified along with the ethereal body during this process. This is how you begin to embody your soul: by making space for it in your purified ethereal body. (See the diagram "Surrendering Ethereal Energy Stages" on page 98.)

Before the experience of being, the soul was only present in the mental body. Now through the condition of being, you can embody the soul in both the mental center and the ethereal center. Calmness, stillness, and a general sense of inner restfulness is the experience of the final stages of the condition of being. that characterizes this stage of development.

To mature the condition of being requires patience and time. You cannot force it! We should not expect to sit in meditation once and immediately grow into the depths of being.

A Purified Ethereal Body

During your final stages of the condition of being, you experience how ethereal energy makes its way out of your physical body, giving you the sensation of growing roots that descend into the ground from the base of our spine. This is a sign that the energy of your ego is being drawn down by the gravity of the Earth, which absorbs it, leaving you with a perception of your energy becoming transparent.

You perceive this new, transparent condition of being in two ways. Primarily, you experience it from the view of the soul, which is guiding the process as it is merging with the purified ethereal body. Secondarily, you experience it from the view of the ego that is surrendering its dominance over you by letting go of all the different kinds of energy you've been attached to that influence the perception of your soul.

The interaction between the soul and the ethereal aspect of the ego concludes when the ego is completely purified and the energy of the soul has taken its place. When your ethereal energy is fully purified, the ethereal aspect of the ego actually does not exist anymore. It has been transformed into the *pure self of being*.

Now, your subjective experience of this refined state of being is recognized as transparence. Once the ethereal body has depleted its "unclean" energy through the root chakra, the soul begins illuminating your ethereal body. This is the optimum condition of being.

During the final stage of being, you fully embody the soul. In essence, this means that you become the soul. You are in total repose within the ethereal dimension and sensing the pure self of being. All ethereal energies are transparent and you are capable of acknowledging the absence of the ethereal aspect of the ego.

At this stage of soul embodiment, if you want to maintain the condition of pure self of being, you need to establish an equilibrium of energy such that you do not go into deeper surrendering. If you engage in a process of deeper surrendering, you will shift into a condition of absence which I will explain in a different chapter.

However, if you do not maintain and adequate pressure of surrendering during this stage, you will return to your previous condition of purification. You will only know about it through practicing.

By learning to maintain equilibrium while surrendering ethereal energy, you can preserve the precious stage of transparent, pure self. You can abide within the unbroken stillness of the now, experiencing the immaculate expression of the existence of the soul within the ethereal body, and this feels incredibly good while it lasts.

Surrendering is an enjoyable activity because, as you surrender, you are giving up on all that does not provide rest to the soul. You are releasing external forces acquired throughout all your existence--all sorts of energy that has accumulated in your ethereal dimension—and you feel lighter and lighter. You feel a sense of increasing relief and joy.

The experience of transparence and full illumination by the soul is a sublime condition, but it is not the ultimate condition that you may achieve through meditation.

Experiencing the Absolute Through the Ethereal Dimension

Surrendering ethereal energy beyond a purified condition of the ethereal body will eventually bring you into direct contact with the source of the creation. This transition occurs when the purified self is at the maximum surrender point in the dimension of presence and close to becoming absent. With your attention hovering above the lower gate of the ethereal body, you are experiencing your existence through being. However, it is possible to traverse this gate to the other side, where you can experience *nonbeing*.

Do not worry. Your physical body will still be seated on the meditation mat. It will not die just because you had this subjective experience of losing your sense of individuality and self-referencing. You can get all that back later on.

During the condition of being, you experience the flow of the ethereal energy throughout your body in the act of purification to embody the soul. By contrast, during the condition of nonbeing, you completely deplete your body of ethereal energy, while directing it through the root chakra. This enables you to register only as a soul into the source of creation.

I use the word *register* to mimic the word *experience* as a human being would. Since the soul does not have a body, it cannot technically have an experience. In this case, the soul is doing the action and there is no perception from the human side.

The condition of nonbeing is the condition of absence from within the physical and ethereal bodies. In this case, it is the expression of consciousness in the absolute only through the ethereal aspect of the soul. It is samadhi registered through the ethereal dimension.

During this particular condition of absence, the body is in repose while the energy flow of the ethereal body is interrupted. The ethereal energy is totally depleted. Meanwhile, the mental body is not detecting any flow of the ethereal energy and as a result acknowledging its condition of absence. At the same time, the void within the mental body is illuminated by the energy of the soul, aka it is *pure consciousness*. During this stage, you are registering as a soul only within the ethereal aspect. It is only a partial absence, however, because it corresponds only to the absence of the ethereal body. Here, you are still under the influence of both the emotional and mental bodies.

If you want to access the dimension of absence through the ethereal body, you have to go beyond the will of the vital force and surrender your fully purified ethereal body. You need to completely reverse the flow of the emerging vital force as it comes into creation. During meditation, the act of deeply surrendering allows you to enter the realm of the unmanifested. Only by going in this direction can you attain the absolute condition, subjectively experiencing the place where the energy of creation is born. This is the origin of everything that exists and where manifestation explodes into form.

In the condition of nonbeing, you are going beyond the gravity of the now and entering unmanifested reality, a dimension where your sense of presence and time vanishes.

Awakening occurs in the dimension of presence. Samadhi occurs in the dimension of absence. Awakening is a realization about who you are. Samadhi is more about reaching unity consciously with the absolute.

If you want to access the absolute through the ethereal dimension, you need to reach the deepest degree of surrendering possible to us as human beings, which corresponds to going beyond the purification of the ethereal body.

The experience of the condition I am calling the pure self of being represents having equilibrium between the purified energy in the ethereal body and the energy of the absolute. When you are in equilibrium, the exchange of energy in your ethereal body is neutral.

When the pure self of being crosses through the bottom gate of the ethereal body, it accesses the absolute. At this point, your consciousness experiences the absence of self from the ethereal body. Your mental body acknowledges that the pure self of your existence has departed; and because it is not there anymore, we experience it as leaving a void in its place. This acknowledgment is the sign that the pure self of being has reached the absolute through the ethereal dimension.

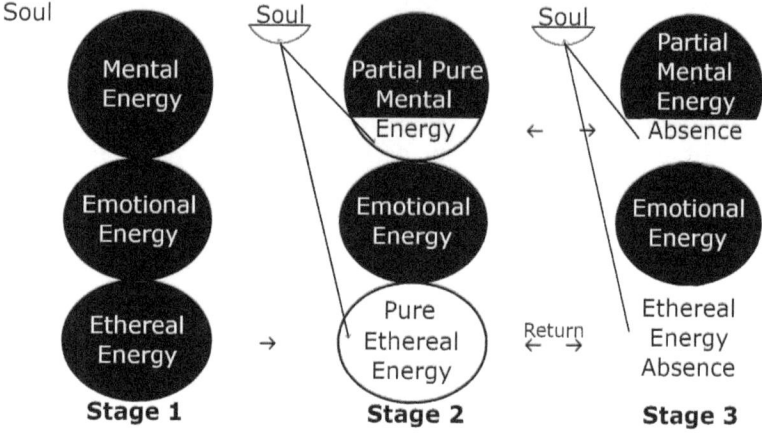

It is important to understand that through the sense of being, you continuously experience the now, while you are transported into a timeless dimension by linking with the absolute. Beyond the door of the root chakra, you make a quantum leap and the soul is absorbed into the absolute.

As I mentioned before, shifting into the absence of being becomes a partial experience of the absolute because at this juncture you can only experience it through the ethereal aspect of the soul. The access to the absolute at this stage goes only as far as the fulfillment of the condition of nonbeing.

Experiencing the soul's existence through the ethereal body is different than experiencing its identity through the mental body. Both the identity and existence of the soul are unique, albeit complementary conditions.

With the act of surrendering to the fullest you can control the ethereal energy and, as a reward, gain access to the absolute condition. The soul feels liberated within the unmanifested realm of the source. Linking with source empowers you to continue to higher levels of spiritual evolution. Ethereal forces are not dominating you any longer because you can apply control over ourselves.

It is an honor to experience the void of creation, a privilege that very few people obtain. To get here, you have to knock at the door located at the bottom of the ethereal soul center and it has to open and let you through, allowing you to explore another dimension of your being. The gate has opened for you to continue our mission and fulfill the purpose of your existence.

Duality Through the Ethereal Dimension

The recognition of duality is very important to accomplish the condition of being and later to transcend into the absolute. Duality, at the ethereal level, is the experience in regards to the existence of the ethereal aspect of the ego and the soul. During this process, the soul continuously interacts with both the mental and ethereal bodies to reach its purification. The ethereal aspect of the ego is the mental portion that acknowledges the existence of the ethereal energy.

The experience of emptiness through the ethereal body challenges physical laws and the usual human mode of perceiving the world. At the instant you subjectively cross the gate from the ethereal body into the absolute the ethereal body becomes absent to our awareness.

It is interesting, however, that the quality of absence registered during this process is incomplete. We can submerge ourselves in the absolute through the ethereal dimension, but despite having this opportunity, you will encounter energetic fluctuations in both our emotional body and your mental body.

Emptiness is a nondual experience; however, because you live in the physical dimension, there is always something in you acknowledging events. Thus, your experiences are dualistic. The only way to fully register emptiness as a nondual condition is by entirely crossing into the absolute through all three soul centers simultaneously. So, if you want to register a deeper quality of absence at this stage, you have to completely isolate the ethereal body.

Stabilizing the Condition of Absence Through the Ethereal Dimension

Human experience will continuously stir up new thoughts, emotions, and physical changes that are mimicked in the ethereal body. It is necessary to continue surrendering and purifying the ethereal soul center throughout your live if you want to nurture the precious treasure that is the soul.

Also, during each meditation practice, after fully surrendering, the ethereal energy will reappear and bring us into a state of presence. This usually happens during our first instant of immersion in the absolute. Our initial entries to the realm of the absolute are unstable, so we may experience casual shifts between the absolute and the final stages of being. For instance, we could fall into absence and suddenly return to the pure self of being. This is normal because the experience of nonexistence is unusual. Most of us were never trained to abide in absence and are used to existing in the physical body—to being.

Entering the absolute is a subtle and sudden experience similar to an implosion of energy. As soon as you deplete the ethereal energy through the root chakra, it disappears increasing the speed of absorption into the source of creation. You are now registering only as a soul in the uncreated through the ethereal aspect because your ethereal energy has merged with creation.

Previously, when having the experience of being, you embodied your soul. But now, at the deepest degree of surrender of ethereal energy, you register your identity as a soul within the absolute.

By continuously surrendering your ethereal energy during meditation, you can stabilize the condition of absence. Falling into the void of the absolute, you are weightless and disappear into complete stillness. You move into a state of unbroken rest. This is how you transcend the ethereal body and merge with the absolute--by entering a transparent, timeless dimension.

When you fall into a fathomless absence and become part of the void of creation, you are capable of having the realization that the ethereal body is not your natural condition, that, in truth, you belong to a different dimension.

The condition of absence at this stage of our spiritual development provides an intimate relation amongst your pure self of being, your soul, and the source of creation. Absence is not a condition of simply managing energy; it is an act of devotion in which you completely surrender your existence.

Without making a commitment to embody the soul and merge with the absolute, surrendering ethereal energy would merely be a physical exercise that lacks the real importance it deserves.

Before you can advance further in your meditations, you will need to learn to stabilize the condition of absence from the ethereal dimension. You will need to be capable of finding your equilibrium and overcoming any fluctuations of energy that you experience. You also need to practice continuous, conscious recognition of your soul. In this way, you can identify the boundaries of your ethereal soul center and learn to perpetually surrender.

You need to be able to isolate the experience of ethereal energy flowing in you from everything else. And then to isolate the experience of its absence.

Until you can isolate the absent condition, you cannot arrive at the experience of pure self of being or enter the absolute through the ethereal dimension.

In brief, you need to master the process of transcending your ethereal body.

Chapter 12

AWAKENING THE EMOTIONAL BODY

Your emotional body is a dimension of much higher frequency energy than the range of energy you experience within the ethereal dimension. This body is an instrument of communication between the physical body, the soul, and the Divine. *The Divine* is the name that people give to the intelligent, nurturing presence they sense when they feel the compassion and love aspects of the absolute. The other term I've been using for this comforting presence throughout the book is *the Beloved.*

Awakening the emotional body is an essential step in accessing our human healing power, and more importantly, the divine essence of our souls. It is through the emotional body that we awaken the divinity within us and get the sublime opportunity to contact the compassion and love of the Beloved.

The emotional body has three sections: an upper, a middle, and a lower section. The upper and lower sections correspond to the throat chakra and the solar plexus chakra, respectively. The middle section encompasses the heart, the thymus gland, and a portion of the lungs. But for the sake of simplicity, we can call it the heart chakra.

In order to become someone who can consciously access the energy of the emotional body, you must be able to create necessary conditions. An energetic safeguard is in place that will stop you from entering without meeting the necessary prerequisites.

Nobody is allowed to get into this sacred place before mastering their ethereal energy. But once you have, you are allowed to knock at the door of the emotional body and wait for it to be opened.

If we want to consciously access the emotional body, it is also necessary to stabilize the condition of absence in the ethereal dimension. We spoke of this at length in the previous chapter. The stabilization of absence in the ethereal dimension requires you to have a fully surrendered ethereal body and to be experiencing the constant presence of the soul. Once these conditions have been achieved, your soul will guide you into and through the dimension of the emotional body.

When entering the emotional body, you find yourself on the path of purification and healing of it, just like we previously purified the ethereal body. After pursuing this path to its end, from there your soul will reveal your connection to the domain of compassion and love.

If you have not awakened your awareness and mastered the ethereal dimension yet, I recommend that you continue practicing the meditation sequence described in the preceding chapter until you are successful in achieving its objectives. Without ethereal mastery, your experience of your emotional body will only translate into emotion without reality.

Let me explain.

Some people believe that when they feel loving and compassionate, they are having a full perception of qualities of a good spiritual being. But this is a misperception. If they do not have the foundation of consciousness or cannot sense the identity of the soul, they will continue to be separated from the reality of the Divine. Even their perception of kindness and caring will be an imitation of something even purer and more refined.

Awareness is pure consciousness reflected in the terrain of our minds. Like a flame casting its glow over everything near it, awareness is how you can ascertain you are in the presence of the soul. Awareness is the soul's illumination of your mental field. Only those embodying the energy of the soul have the capacity to calm their minds and access the intimate depths of their emotional bodies.

Any attempt to enter your emotional dimension before having established an identity beyond the ego personality is unmanageable and worthless. However, if you have the clarity of awareness and continuity of presence, then you are ready to carry the light of the soul that entered you through the ethereal realm into the emotional body to begin its transformation.

The complete realization of the emotional body entails three important stages: purification, healing, and merging with the Divine.

To explain the complete realization of the emotional body, I divide each stage into two parts. The first part refers to the interpretation of our emotional perceptions within daily activities. The second part is the corresponding inner energetic work done during meditation.

Purification of the Emotional Body

Purification of your emotional energy is a process that begins with freeing the mind from the influence of negative impulses that create barriers in your emotional body to alignment with your soul. For example, when you are emotionally hurt you might create barriers of protection in similar situations to avoid pain in the future.

During the purification stage of realization, we release all protective emotional barriers acquired during our lives so that we can align with the purpose of the soul.

The work of emotional purification starts once you are connected to your soul. The emotional aspect of the ego is unable to clean itself because it is always trying to find ways to protect its own existence. To succeed, an entity more powerful than the ego has to transform it. You have to allow your higher self to enter your body and, from there, to mobilize the light of your real nature. Only your soul, along with universal consciousness, can purify the subconscious tendencies in you that create barriers affecting the emotional body and its alignments.

The mind (which governs the emotional body) cannot purify itself because it will always find new ways to protect its imperfections. Only the soul is able to purify and heal the imperfect. The soul can help you achieving the purification process because it exists in a perfect dimension where it is flooded with the light of the source. There is a very limited amount of work that the emotional mind can do without being in the presence of the soul. The soul's presence can dismantle stagnant energy that is affecting your mental and emotional body guiding you through purification and healing.

Emotional Duality

Duality, at the emotional level, is the experience in regards to the existence of the emotional aspect of the ego and the soul. During this process, the soul continuously interacts with both the mental and emotional bodies to reach its purification. The emotional aspect of the ego is the mental portion that acknowledges the existence of the emotional energy.

Like the duality we experienced during the awakening of consciousness, this second time, we perceive emotional duality when we identify with the emotional aspect of the ego and not with the soul. Remember you are not your body, you are not your emotions and you are not your or mind, you are your soul.

You, as a soul, are represented by your awakened consciousness. The ego emotional self is represented by the portion of the mental body acknowledging the flow of emotional energy and the emotional energy itself

When ego emotional aspect trusts the soul and follows its guidance in the process of surrendering, then purification begins. That's the catalyst. Next, the ego emotional aspect starts to vanish and eventually our perception of emotional duality disappears.

The Center of Emotion

If you want to reveal the truth of the emotional body, you need to recognize your emotions as the main ingredient flowing within your emotional body. The emotions of many people exercise exceptional command over their minds, dictating their thoughts, intentions, and actions. It is not uncommon to find some highly sensitive people who act by impulse and, most of the time, are controlled by their feelings. They are so easily affected by their emotions that their desires and upsets often undermine their capacity for making rational decisions.

Heart and mind are intimately attached and can easily influence one another. The emotional body may express negative tendencies that originate in the mind. When you have negative thoughts, you feel negative emotions. And it is a two-way street: Likewise, negative emotions can produce negative thoughts. For this reason, it is very important to know how you process your emotions.

As you live, the sensations of different emotions arise in your physical body. Given sufficient experience, you may or may not determine how to manage or control them effectively. Most of the time, if you study what's going on objectively, you will learn that your emotions are not based on real facts but are the products of erroneous perceptions or conclusions you've arrived at mentally.

It is important to pay careful attention to your emotions. If they are not being received through your emotional body but have originated without tangible evidence to back them up, then your subjective interpretations of events may be causing false consequences of joy or pain.

Many people end up hurting themselves, experiencing feelings of shame and guilt without realizing that these feelings are byproducts of their own imaginations.

It is important to understand that you can originate emotions within your mind—and also to recognize that you cannot feel emotions within your mind. This distinction is significant.

For instance, mentally driven people have developed their intelligence to the point that they only trust their heads in guiding their daily activities. They try only to use principles of logic to respond to their emotions, and will act in accordance to morality, principles, or situations.

We can see mentally driven people processing anger, hate, or love in their heads while not feeling it from the real place that it manifests, their emotional bodies.

While most of us know people who consider their feelings the most important part of their lives, no doubt we also know others who are less concerned with them. Or who are even more identified with the physical and mental aspects of life.

In general, mentally oriented people create barriers to emotion in order to avoid being hurt. They do not give emotions access to their hearts. Emotionally oriented people do not have such barriers and are dominated by their emotions because they are unable to regulate them. Both types of people represent extremes. These modes of living are not useful except in rare contexts. Mainly, they are obstacles that keep people separated from the divinity of their soul.

Some people think that being highly sensitive gives them more access to their souls; however, a sensitive disposition without consciousness is a horrible mix that will take anyone in the opposite direction of the soul.

Allowing Free Flow of Emotions

The first stage in purification of the emotional body is allowing for a free flow of emotion without any barriers. This is not an easy task, particularly when we are experiencing pain. Here, I refer to normal situations that occur in daily life. Later, I will explain how to allow free flow of emotions during your meditation practice.

When defending against being hurt, we create psychological barriers. It is a natural human behavior to create a system in the mind to filter out emotional pain and hardship, such as we might feel in traumatic situations. But we also can have barriers against routine things like intimacy. Apparently, many of us find it risky to be emotionally vulnerable and will create shields to avoid being hurt by loss or disappointment or even for the more narcissistic aim of looking different ("better") than we are. Anxiety can lead to total emotional shutdown—depression.

The reality is that it does not matter how we defend ourselves from our internal responses to the exterior world; we will still be susceptible to being hurt. Being vulnerable is an inherent condition. We are born vulnerable, with an immense capacity to be hurt as we live our lives. And at the end, we still die being vulnerable. There is nothing that can completely protect us from our vulnerability.

We need to accept vulnerability because it allows us to see life from this different perspective.

Of course, accepting vulnerability does not mean that we should desire pain or become masochists, only that we are ready to face pain instead of avoiding it. If we try to avoid suffering, we will repress and store a large number of feelings somewhere in our physical bodies. One day, this burden could make us collapse.

When a reservoir is at its maximum fullness, it cannot contain more water. The gates of its dam must be opened to release the pressure on its walls. As soon as the gates open, the river resumes its course and the pressure is relieved. Similarly, when you open the gate of your heart chakra and let your pain flow freely, you are relieved of pressure from your pent-up emotions.

Unless we learn how to let ourselves flow with pain, we are not going to survive it. We should not avoid pain by diverting it into different activities. Instead, we should go towards it without putting up any resistance or barriers.

The more you try to avoid pain, the more you will find yourself in pain because this way reinforces pain.

When feeling pain, you need to realize that your suffering is a signal telling you that something is going wrong within you. Perhaps you are holding onto something from the past that you need to release.

For this reason, you have to be vigilant all the time and not let the mind erect barriers. You should not resist pain or protect against vulnerability because it is there that you find the quickest route to evolving into the divinity of your soul.

As long as you remain in the physical dimension, you will have to deal with pain because it is a normal and unavoidable aspect of life. It is by getting acquainted with pain, by accepting it instead of repelling it, that you begin your emotional transformation. When we change our perceptions of pain and create a positive relationship with it, we can begin the process of purification. If you will allow your painful emotions to flow freely, the events that triggered them could become your greatest teachers.

You need to begin dismantling any protective walls you've created to defend your heart chakra because, at the end of the day, this shielding is eclipsing your divine capacity for compassion and love.

We need to trust the soul and promise to tear down all barriers and let emotions pour into the emotional soul center without any resistance. The mental portion of the emotional self (ego) needs to surrender. In its surrendering, all blockages are dissolved and a free flow of emotions into the heart chakra is initiated.

You need to take apart your defense structures so you may recover the sensibility you lost in the center of your emotional body. It is time to reclaim it by relinquishing all defenses that make you callous. Then, through your vulnerability, you can access the divinity of your soul and encounter real compassion and love.

Do not try to avoid vulnerability because your barriers will keep you confined. It is fundamental to drop any obsession you feel about protecting your image. Drop the shields fabricated by your mind and let your soul guide you through a quest.

The Impact of the Mind on Our Emotional Body

The second stage of purifying the emotional body is to dissolve the thinking that affects it.

Very often you add extra mental energy to your pain, which increases it. When you layer extra mental energy on top of an initial pain, you end up adversely affecting your physical, psychological, and spiritual well-being. If you can learn how to relate to undesirable situations more effectively, you can avoid unnecessary additional pressure in your lives.

It is the ego emotional-self represented by the mind that very often contributes extra pain into the mix of our lives. You need to be attentive by not allowing the mind to fabricate thoughts that can end up adding self-inflicted pain to your lives.

Here's an example of how this works. If, for any reason, you are experiencing psychological pain, there is a possibility that you find yourself experiencing physical pain as well. This happens because you cannot manage the psychological pain and end up transferring it into your physical body. Or the opposite happens: You have physical pain and it affects you emotionally.

I will tell a short story to explain. This morning when I was walking down the stairs, I fell and hit my knee on the floor. Now I am feeling pain in my knee. Looking closely at this injury in retrospect, there was only physical pain.

Later today, in the afternoon, I was sitting on a chair thinking about how terrible my knee feels and how unlucky and upset I am because an injury happened to me. As we can see, the event has evolved to include an extra dimension of experience. I transformed the purely physical pain of the event into psychological pain.

Any addition to our memory of the physical accident is an unnecessary elaboration by our mind.

On top of telling myself that new story, perhaps created to alleviate the initial pain or both the physical and psychological pain, I decide to eat and watch television in an attempt to forget the incident. The pleasure of eating and watching television was delightful; however, when I finished this mind-numbing activity, both my physical and my psychological discomfort came back. At that point, I needed a more powerful counteracting agent to soothe my pain.

This final self-soothing event—whatever it ended up being—was an example of what happens when we try to avoid pain.

The example above may not be perfect, but the conclusion is: We understand that we cannot avoid physical pain, but we can create a better relationship to pain by accepting it and remaining more detached from it. Furthermore, we cannot be free from psychological pain, but we can minimize it by avoiding additional suffering generated by our mind.

Pain is a natural occurrence. The problem is not the pain itself or our inability to avoid it but much more the mental outlook that we adopt towards emotion. It is up to us how we approach pain, and it is also an option if we want to further hurt ourselves.

Agreement to Surrender

Surrendering emotional barriers and controlling the effect the mind has on the emotional body requires us to establish daily regimen of coherent behavior paired with our meditation practice. Coherent behavior and a meditation practice are complementary activities that support us in our spiritual evolution. They will help us to transform into a pure and complete emotional self by aligning our human identity with the higher intention of the soul.

Maintaining coherent behavior patterns entails taking responsibility for your emotions and their interaction with your minds. Coherent behavior is ignited by the presence of the soul. It is consciousness that sparks understanding of the true nature of your existence.

And I am not referring to behavior of following norms of conduct or social practices but much more the one that we adopt in accordance to the principles of the soul.

Coherent behavior is the result of surrendering to your soul with the intention to purify your emotional body. If you want to purify the emotional body, you need to set a clear intention to accomplish this objective. It is simply not enough to be in contact with your emotional body. The ego needs to share a clear intention to yield to the presence of the soul. The emotional portion of the human mind needs to surrender to agree with the soul so that purification can proceed.

For this to happen, you need to recognize the presence of the soul. Without the presence of the soul there is not a valid surrendering process. The ego aspect of the emotional body has to acknowledge and surrender to the presence of the soul. This is how the ego emotional self makes a firm commitment to the soul, letting it take command over it. Only when the ego emotional self accepts the supremacy of the soul does purification begin.

The emotional ego cannot purify or heal itself because it is imperfect. It needs the power of the soul to purify it. But it does not want to surrender because it fears disappearing. It will always find ways to justify its existence and, left to its own devices, will continue neglecting purification and healing. In surrendering to the soul, however, the emotional body recovers its original sensitivity and you find perfect harmony to serve the purposes of the soul.

Doing Inner Energetic Work to Purify the Emotional Body

The inner work of the emotional body begins with the purification of the emotional body in the solar plexus chakra, which is where an energetic battle between mind and emotions takes place.

During this stage of purification, you surrender all the barriers of emotional protection you set during your life so that you can allow free flow of emotion into your emotional body.

Surrendering within the emotional soul center takes place during meditation by going directly into your inner energetic field. You have to access and take control over the raw energy flowing within your emotional body to be successful.

Let us remember that the emotional soul center has three components: the solar plexus, heart, and throat chakras. Energetic recognition of these three components is important if we want to access our emotional energy.

The emotional energy flow is more concentrated in the area of the solar plexus chakra, at the bottom section of the emotional body. This is the point in which we need to focus our attention at the beginning of this practice.

The solar plexus chakra exchanges energy in two directions. One-way, emotional energy flows towards the interior of our bodies, the other way emotional energy flows towards the external world. The solar plexus chakra is the gate that we use to surrender within the emotional soul center.

Similar to the other centers of the soul, within the emotional soul center the energy flows in two directions. Looking at it from an upright position, the flow goes down from the throat chakra to the heart chakra and them to the solar plexus chakra at the front side and inside the body. The flow goes up from the solar plexus chakra to the heart chakra and them to the throat chakra at the back side and inside of the body. The energy flow within the emotional soul center is similar to water vapor.

The first step during the surrendering process is to recognize the flow of energy within the emotional soul center.

During the practice of meditation, after having awakened and stabilized the ethereal body, you can begin detecting the energetic flow of your emotional soul center.

As you focus attention on your solar plexus chakra, you may begin experiencing a fluctuation of energy entering your emotional body. Initially you may detect this movement as a subtle vibration; later it transforms into an exchange of energy flow being distributed through the center of the body into both the ethereal and emotional soul centers.

Since the solar plexus chakra operates as a transition point between the emotional and ethereal bodies; your consciousness can approach and enter your emotional body either by coming to it directly from the ethereal body or by coming to it from the condition of absence from the absolute.

It is preferable not to abide for a long time at the level of the solar plexus because it is a place of heavy energy exchange. It is better to continue moving with the energy that is flowing towards the heart chakra.

When you are able to sense the energy flow within the emotional soul center, you can begin merging with it.

The sensation becomes intense as you subjectively begin flowing into that energetic field going upwards into the center of the emotional body however you still need to continue sensing the flow of energy going downwards.

SURRENDERING EMOTIONAL BODY ENERGY

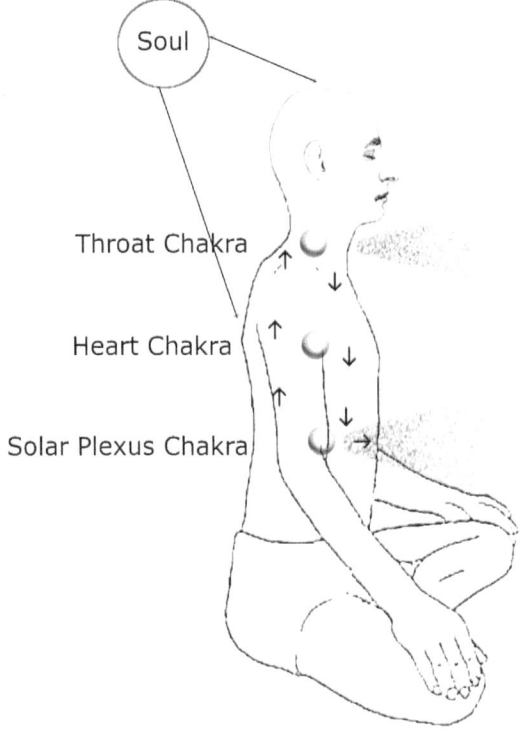

Initially the energy coming from the heart chakra is more intense than the energy moving in the opposite direction. You may notice that when approaching your heart chakra, you are repelled by waves of resistance.

These energy waves coming from the heart chakra correspond to the barriers of protection you created throughout your life.

You need to overcome the repelling waves of energy from your heart chakra by surrendering energy through the front flow going downwards and at the same time by merging with the weaker flow that goes towards the heart chakra. This is how you begin the process of purification within the emotional soul center.

Before I continue explaining this practice, I believe I must pause to highlight the participation of the mental body during the process of surrendering within the emotional soul center.

Besides surrendering emotional energy, a portion of the mental body must also surrender to facilitate purification.

The portion of the mental body that needs to surrender corresponds to the ego that created the emotional barriers of protection which is the portion of the mind acknowledging the presence and functioning of the emotional body.

As you breathe, with each inhalation you can increase the flow of energy going upwards to your heart chakra, and with each exhalation you can displace painful sensations going downwards to your solar plexus chakra. It is by letting go of thoughts and surrendering your emotional will that you begin purifying and embodying your soul.

Without the joint participation of the ego emotional aspect and the presence of the soul you could not proceed to surrender.

When entering the emotional soul center, you need to keep the presence of the soul while the mind continuously rests and surrenders. The more that you relax your mind, the easier you will flow into the emotional energy.

We begin the process of surrendering within the emotional soul center by overcoming the energetic waves that prevents us from approaching the heart chakra and by pushing that energy towards the solar plexus chakra.

Initially, the experience of approaching the center of the emotional body may feel like a heavy, uncomfortable sensation. The barriers of protection coming from the heart are strong so we need to remove them slowly. If you rush doing it, the uncomfortable sensation increases with pain.

It is here that you must start the backbreaking mission of purifying the emotional body. By displacing the protection barriers that provide uncomfortable sensation downwards through the solar plexus, you can begin regulating the quality and quantity of emotional energy that is entering your heart chakra.

You are making room for yourself to get closer to your heart chakra. You are clearing away all barriers that block the free flow of your emotions.

While you overcome and surrender this energetic field, your mental body is surrendering as well therefore contributing to its continuous stabilization. In fact, these barriers of emotional protection were created by the mental body so we need to surrender with them.

At the beginning, approaching the heart chakra is difficult. You will experience discomfort because you are releasing all kinds of emotional barriers that you've accumulated during your lifespan. When you release the opposing flow of energy within your emotional body, you purify the path and make it possible for fresh, free-flowing emotions to enter your spiritual heart.

The blocking energy you surrender helps you aligning your human condition with the purpose of the soul. As you approach the center of the emotional body, you are getting ready to enter into your heart chakra.

The surrendered, steam-like energy that moves out of the emotional body through your solar plexus chakra leaves a clear path behind within which to process your stale old thoughts and sensations.

The purification process is complete when you have surrendered all the barriers of emotional protection. You will notice it when there is no more resistance while approaching the heart chakra.

There is not a clear division to determine the completion of this stage and the following healing process only until you enter the heart chakra.

Healing the Emotional Body

Healing the emotional body requires the deep surrender of emotional energy, a dynamic process in which you prepare to experience the divinity of the soul. During the healing period, you transform your emotional relationship with suffering. It is a phase in which you recover from traumatic experiences that have wounded you by transforming your human suffering into love and unity under the guidance of the soul.

Following emotional healing, you become able to find your original sense within the emotional dimension. You become at one with the emotional energy in your heart chakra. Initially, it was when you awakened the ethereal body that you identified with the soul. During this new stage, you start sensing as your soul within your purified emotional body. You are evolving into the "I am" of love and compassion within the middle of your emotional soul center.

Emotional healing is only possible when we fully surrender our emotions to the soul. A purified and healed ethereal body is the maximum spiritual evolution that we can experience in the emotional body before merging with the absolute through the emotional dimension.

Trust Is the Foundation of Healing

If we want to transform the emotional body, we need to have absolute trust in the soul. The presence of the soul is insufficient in itself to accomplish our healing. Trusting your soul is the foundation of the process.

The soul has to become the most important aspect of your life. It has to consciously become the essence of your existence. By trusting in the soul, you acquire a sensation of completeness, clarity, confidence, and love. If you do not trust, you always have a sense of separation, uncertainty, and fear instead.

Trust in the soul begins when you surrender your emotional barriers with the intention of serving the soul. Repeatedly doing so during your meditation sessions is how the ego emotional self gradually is purified and healed. The deepest form of emotional trust in the soul happens when you fully surrender to its presence. Then, the ego emotional self disappears and you begin acting from your soul and continuously expressing it.

The Energy of Emotion

Throughout our lives, we build a self-image according to experiences and sensations that arise during our interactions with our surroundings. One time, we identify with one emotion. The next, we identify with another one. We think, "I am an angry person," "I am a happy person," "I am a grieving person," and so forth. We may associate with an emotion provided by a relationship, work, or religion, then later we do not associate with it because it is less important to us.

Emotions contribute to shaping our personalities; however, anything that we identify with turns into an influence that motivate us. It becomes a force that eclipses the light of our real self, inhibiting our ability to perceive it.

When we identify with an emotion, we are blocking the opportunity to have other sensations. That emotion becomes the essence of our life and we mistakenly believe it is us. We may feel emotions and have ideas that overtake us with their intensity but none is who we really are. Our real identity exists in a dimension of the soul beyond thoughts and emotions.

We need emotions to express ourselves and exist as human beings in the world; however, when we identify with them, we become their prisoners. They will control us.

We need to create a condition in which we can find our real sensibility within the emotional dimension. We need to make room for the soul to be embodied within the emotional body.

During the awakening of the ethereal body, you established the presence of the soul in the ethereal dimension. Now that you are working with the emotional body, you can follow a similar plan. you need to surrender enough emotional energy to establish the presence of your soul in the emotional body. By surrendering emotions one after the other, you may start disassociating from them and healing the emotional body.

Associating with emotions is an aspect of the human condition. You think of positive emotions as indicators of prosperity. You think of negative emotions as threats to your existence in the physical world.

You may enjoy positive emotions and be uncomfortable with negative emotions; however, you need to approach both types of emotions in the same manner. you need to understand that emotions are only experiences you have during your existence. They are not you. You need to experience emotions but should never identify with any of them.

In general, emotions are associated with the outside world. You need to eliminate external influences on the emotional body and surrender every emotion that arises. By surrendering, you tap into the inner universe of light and love and begin healing your emotional condition. It is your soul that provides you with the assurance, empowerment, and love you need to believe that you are erroneously looking outside.

After you surrender all your emotions, you will discover the pure self of the emotional body and awaken your heart chakra. You will also return to a state of innocence and experience the pure, peaceful feeling of your existence. This how you can experience the authentic sense of you without the influence of the external world.

When you empty yourself of emotional impurities, you allocate space to go deeper into your heart chakra. You are filled with a warm sense of love and safety, and you create a suitable condition to awaken the divine sense of the soul.

Most people do not know how to surrender and easily make the mistake of identifying with their emotions. But if you identify with your emotions, you will find yourself in a world of emotions and there won't be anything else around you. Emotions and only emotions!

For instance, when feeling pain, you will look around in the world of emotions to counteract that pain because you identified with it. You will feel urgency to neutralize it with pleasure, but when the remedy disappears, pain will impact you again. When feeling happiness, you look forward to continuing to be happy because you identify with it too.

Trying to escape pain is a common practice of those submerged with emotion because they will look for the cure in pleasure as the only escape from pain or uncomfortable experiences. They do not know another way to heal from it because they haven't yet experienced the healing power of their souls.

Usually, people immersed in emotion feel and think erroneously because they are not able to see their real connection. They are too disconnected from their souls and the absolute.

Asking someone who has not experienced the energy of the soul to disassociate from thoughts and emotion is probably a waste of time. They may be so lost within thoughts and emotion that they are not able to perceive it. They experience the same sensation as a fish does in water. Fish are not capable of distinguishing water from the air that lies beyond it because they require water for their survival. People who have not awakened their awareness cannot tell the difference between the mind and the soul.

When you have the presence of the soul, you can perceive emotion and thoughts as separate from our identity and this initiates the process of surrendering within the emotional body. As we surrender, we can go beyond emotion and thoughts and meet our soul within our spiritual heart.

It is the soul that heals us emotionally. When surrendering, we let our mind rest from thinking and reviewing thoughts and sensations. Then our soul takes over and empties out our pain and negativity. We just rest and let go.

Realizing how memories and emotions came into our lives is a purely psychological exercise. Psychological exercises are insufficient to embody the soul and merge with the absolute because they cause us to reaffirm emotional behaviors and reinforce the presence of emotional memoires.

The more that you think about certain emotions, the more you fix them in your mind. No matter how much you try fixing these experiences utilizing only your mind, you cannot.

We, as human beings, need to experience the world through sensations and thoughts but not by identifying with them. For instance, we must perceive being rich, poor, powerful, weak, and so on, as a temporary condition that we created within our journey as a human being. We must see how it only exists within the transient physical dimension.

Because we are eternal, anything transient is not what we really are! Our true self exists beyond that condition. We are emanations of the force that radiates throughout everything in creation and not our own creations. We may be creators of certain conditions but we are never any condition itself.

When we understand this distinction, we are beyond these conditions and advance into the process of healing.

Realization of the Heart Chakra

Sensing the heart chakra is different than sensing the human heart. For one thing, it doesn't beat or circulate blood because it isn't a muscle. The heart chakra is the divine dimension of the soul that holds compassion and the power of true love.

We need to shift into a higher dimension to experience the heart chakra and allow the divine identity of the soul to unfold.

We need to heal the emotional body to access the spiritual heart. During the process of healing our emotional body, we release each memory and emotion that enters our heart chakra. You might imagine that during this task we are avoiding emotions or bypassing our memories; paradoxically, we are facing and releasing them. We cannot experience the reality of the heart chakra without releasing memories and emotions.

By allowing the free flow of emotions and releasing them, we transform our emotional body and purify the heart chakra. The beauty is how it transforms our emotional identity. We experience ourselves as the "I am" of the heart chakra. This is a very subtle perception.

The heart chakra and the human heart are interconnected but exist in overlapping, parallel dimensions. The human heart is connected with personality while the heart chakra is detached from personality. The human heart experiences the core sense of emotions while the heart chakra experiences the pure sense of divinity.

After our "I am" enters our spiritual heart, we will continue to be linked to our emotional body, however we will also begin sensing emotions in a different manner. In the past, we experienced emotions in reference to the external world; now we identify them subjectively. We start processing sensations in a different pattern because they flow freely through our emotional body and mind without affecting them. We achieve a condition of neutrality.

This would probably seem very strange to some people because it is counter to the conventional way in which they live. A common belief is that the more emotional you get the more sensitive and spiritual you are.

The experience of the heart chakra occurs outside any psychological context. It is a condition in which the emotional mind and body are free from any clamor or hesitation because there is no self-identification with emotions. In this condition, we do not operate from the mind; we operate from the inner realm, a divine place of serenity and wisdom associated with the soul.

To risk repeating myself, the only way to experience the heart chakra is by healing the emotional body. Healing is a stage in which the emotional body becomes pure and transparent because we have reached the highest degree of vibration possible within the emotional body.

A healed emotional body experiences clarity. This is the experience of emotional subjectivity. The sense of what we really are without the influence of the external world.

What are the benefits of this new, soulful condition? A purified and healed emotional body corresponds to the highest realization of a human with the expression of the soul through the emotional dimension. You have surrendered to the intention of the soul and acquired the pure sense of your identity into the heart chakra.

It is important to know that with a purified and healed emotional body; you still can experience physical pain as other humans do. However, your psychological pain is different than that of others because it only arises as a response in the present and it contains compassion for the world.

You do not get pain as a chain reaction from mental activity because common desirable things do not captivate your mind and undesirable ones do not provoke any resistance in you. If you have reached this point, you have already learned how to keep a quiet mind and remain free from compulsive tendencies because your existence is infused with the light of the soul. You act fearlessly because you have nothing to lose and are completely committed to the higher intention of your soul.

The deepest purification and healing of the emotional body is the realization of the heart chakra, which involves the union of awareness and love. It is a complete soul illumination of your emotional body on Earth. It is the connection with the Divine expression of the soul that allows us to release all sense of separateness and fear.

During this stage of our spiritual maturation, we completely isolate the emotional body. It is a condition of emotional subjectivity, a dimension wherein our emotional body does not experience influences from thoughts or other external agents. Our heart chakra is healed and is sensing the purity of the soul beyond the human emotions.

It is a condition of pure sensitivity with the sense of tenderness and transparence expanding all around our existence.

Wisdom and Compassion

Consciousness is very important for our spiritual evolution; however, it is only complete when united with love. Consciousness alone will always be incomplete and never be enough to transform the human personality. Equally, love by itself will never be sufficient to serve our spiritual evolution.

When consciousness meets love, we reach a new level in our evolution. We obtain a deep spiritual realization because the union of consciousness and love brings us wisdom and a sense of abiding compassion.

Also, it is important to differentiate knowledge from wisdom. While knowledge is the perception about the world recognized by the five senses, wisdom is the product of being wise through the progress of the soul. Wisdom is more than just knowledge, cleverness. Wisdom goes beyond the mere act of reasoning because it encompasses an intuitive perception of the truth.

Wisdom is the result of an advanced realization of consciousness, while compassion is the true expression of love. It is through the union of compassion and wisdom that we may create stability in our spiritual heart.

The realization of consciousness and love in the heart chakra is the power from our soul to govern our existence and emotions. This is the maximum actualization of the soul possible in the heart chakra within the human existence. The source of consciousness and love is the absolute.

Consciousness and compassion cannot exist alone because they depend on each other. Hypothetically, consciousness without compassion would turn someone destructive and compassion without consciousness would induce someone to lose control and direction. But they coexist.

Consciousness and compassion reaffirm our identity with the soul. There is not enough consciousness without love and there is not enough compassion without consciousness. Consciousness and compassion are the main components of the soul reflected in the human identity.

Before we can feel compassion, we need to sense the pain that causes that compassion and this may only be perceived deep in the spiritual heart. Self-love and compassion reside in the heart chakra not in the mind. It is the heart chakra that tells the mind to cherish other living beings and wishes they were released from their suffering.

Compassion is not an idea experienced in the mind. And it cannot be dictated by social or ethical norms. We may have learned at school to behave in a compassionate manner; however, that is not enough to understand it. It is only when we experience compassion in our hearts that we really know what compassion is.

Genuine compassion is universal and not only a feeling of good will toward our family and friends or neighbors. Real compassion is something we feel toward all sentient beings.

We need to go deep into our heart chakra to increase the scope of our love and compassion. We have to begin with self-compassion, which is necessary to heal our ego emotional self. Then we may progress deeper into our heart chakra and recognize universal compassion.

Wisdom and compassion are fully recognized when we are merging with our heart chakra. Perhaps one of the most difficult undertakings for some people working with the emotional body is to consciously distinguish between the physical heart and the heart chakra. The heart chakra is not the energy field of the human heart. The heart chakra belongs to the soul. It just happens to be located in a dimension parallel to the physical heart—in the region of the chest. And it is here where we find the origin of love.

Within the heart chakra we find a space of absolute tenderness where silence and stillness merge with the original sensation of love. By being conscious, as a presence, within our spiritual heart, we can recognize the genuine existence of love. The heart chakra is a sacred place where wisdom and compassion form a perfect unity.

Compassion is the main catalyst for surrendering. With compassion, we can forgive others and ourselves for all that has happened in the past. Forgiveness is the power that releases our pain.

By forgiving, we are not agreeing with the past or condoning it; we are freeing ourselves from the burden and hard sensation of carrying it with us energetically. We are making room in the emotional body to allow the presence of the soul to enter and merge with us.

When we forgive, we give up on painful sensations. When we let go of thoughts and emotions we surrender our emotional energy, we begin resting and uniting with the one that allows us to feel (the soul).

When we relinquish emotional energy, we can heal and experience the supreme love and luminosity of the soul. By removing all impurities from the emotional body, we become capable of receiving the virtues of the soul. If we do not extract all painful energy, the emotional body won't be able to receive our soul's light in the heart.

So, every moment that we surrender helps us develop a capacity to be free from pain. It helps us relinquish our will to the soul's. This practice applies for both during the routine of life and during meditation.

During the act of releasing pain, we are not ignoring but experiencing it. Without going through it, we would not be able to know who really exists behind that pain. We must immerse ourselves deeply into the impurities in the heart chakra to experience both the pain and its release.

Doing Inner Energetic Work to Heal the Emotional Body

The energetic work to heal the emotional body is a continuation from its previous stage of purification. There is not a definitive separation between the two stages. The healing stage is a deeper surrender of emotional and mental energy while entering the heart chakra.

By traveling deeper into the center of the emotional body as we continuously surrender, you can finally enter the heart chakra. The experience of this is a burning sensation and a lifting of a warm flow of energy. That flow is the raw ingredient of our emotions entering the heart chakra.

At this time, the presence of the soul becomes stronger because the barriers that were upsetting you melt down and you start recovering your original sensibility. Some people experience entering of the heart chakra as a burning, painful sensation while others perceive it with profound sadness. After all, the heart chakra has been locked for a long time by its insensibility filters and now it is recovering its ability to sense.

The sensation of energy pouring into your heart chakra becomes more intense as you go deeper and it will progress until you completely enter your heart chakra.

The discomfort when entering your heart chakra will stay for some time, and the duration depends on each individual. After some time, the pain or sadness caused from this event will finally disappear.

When I mention pain, I mean pain precisely! We are sensing the raw energetic pain that is the residue of our emotional wounds.

We should not force it or despair about its existence, instead, during each meditation session, we need to approach the heart chakra with tender feeling and love trusting that, in due time, it will heal. We need to go with the flow of energy inside and continue surrendering. The uncomfortable sensation will evaporate through the solar plexus and it will never influence our soul again. It is like a block of ice has melted.

The nonexistence of barriers blocking the flow of emotions through the emotional body ultimately delivers you back into your pure innocence. You begin sensing your real authenticity which is delivered to you by the truth of the spiritual heart. You can now experience your own essence because you do not have any obstacles hiding your sensitivity.

When you completely surrender your emotional barriers, a heavy flow of emotions is released, overflowing the ego emotional self. Your heart chakra is released from the core shield protection of the ego, and now you can bring back and feel your original purity.

Entering your heart chakra is not an easy task. It may take some time before you can do it. Do not zero in with your mind on the heart chakra because the mind can be prejudicial. There ought not to be any reason to rush to access the heart chakra or desperately force the removal of any barriers. We must be patient and kind to ourselves as we approach our heart chakra consciously with devotion and love.

Be aware, your mind spent a reasonable amount of time creating these barriers of protection, so it may take a comparable amount of time to undo them. Establishing conditions of safety and relaxation is appropriate.

The key to healing the emotional body is working consistently on letting go of any sense of achievement or nonachievement so that you can eliminate any blockages stopping the flow of feeling into your heart chakra. Work consciously with tenderness and devotion, and soon you will be in touch with the divinity of your soul. When you reach a certain degree of purification, your heart chakra begins feeling itself independently from us paying attention to it.

We can realize a completely purified and healed emotional body when our heart chakra becomes a self-regulated. Previously, we processed external impressions in the mind, filtering and blocking emotions from reaching our heart chakra. Now we can feel with the heart chakra without misinterpretation or mentally causing changes to our perceptions.

With purification and healing, the emotional body becomes transparent and a pure reflection of the soul. This is how you embody your soul.

Experiencing the Absolute Through the Emotional Dimension

The full realization of the emotional body corresponds to merging our emotional energy with the absolute. This stage corresponds to your second entrance into the realm of the absolute. The first time you reached the absolute through the ethereal dimension; this time, you do it through the emotional dimension.

Let us remember that the absolute is the source of everything. It is the source of creation, love, and consciousness. By entering the absolute through the emotional dimension, you are merging with the divine aspect of the absolute the source of love.

Awakening the emotional body is more about recovering your pure and original sensibility, while entering the absolute through the emotional dimension is about reaching unity with the universal source of love.

When entering the absolute through the emotional dimension, you find the place where the energy of tenderness and love is born.

You need to purify and heal the emotional body to completely reverse its energetic flow. It is only by fully surrendering your emotional energy that you can reach the necessary conditions to cross the bottom gate of your emotional center into the realm of absence. You need to separate your emotional sense to transcend the human emotional condition. You have to go beyond a purified and healed emotional body to experience emotional subjectivity.

Before entering the absolute, you embodied the soul in your emotional body. Now, you can experience your authentic essence within a purified emotional body. You can sense natural love in your heart without any reference with the external world.

Just before entering the absolute, equilibrium is reached between the purified energy of your emotional body and the energy beyond your solar plexus chakra. If you keep surrendering, the pure, healed emotional energy will continue to move out through the solar plexus chakra, crossing the boundary of the realm of the absolute and dissolving.

Through each exhalation of relaxed breath, you continuously dive from your heart chakra down into the depths of the solar plexus gate, finding total rest. Finally, through one deepest breath, you will vanish through that door and merge with the absolute.

SURRENDERING EMOTIONAL ENERGY STAGES

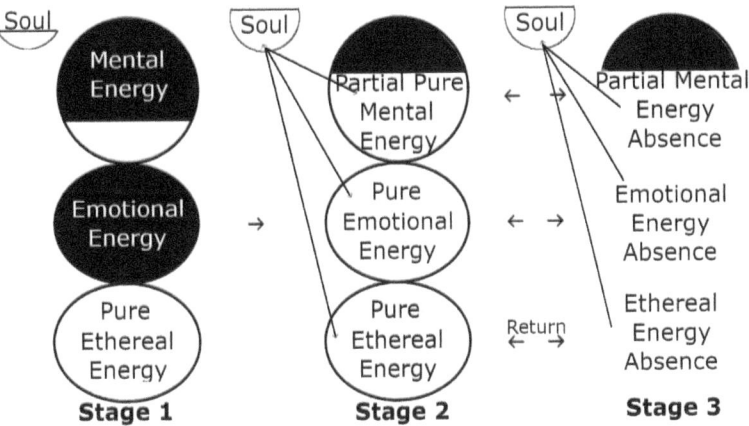

Throughout this stage of absence, the body is in repose while the energy flows into the ethereal and emotional bodies are interrupted. Soon, the energy of the ethereal body and the emotional body is entirely depleted. Once the mental body cannot detect any flow of either ethereal or emotional energy, it acknowledges their absence. The void of absence within the mental body is then illuminated with the energy of the soul.

During this stage of the meditation, we are registering as a soul only within the emotional aspect. It is an advanced condition because it corresponds to the absence of both the ethereal and emotional energy; however, this condition is a partial experience of absence because we are still under the presence of the mental body.

Here, we have transcended the emotional body and merged with the divine source of love in the absolute. There is no sadness or happiness. There is not pain or ecstasy. There is no emotion or nonemotion. There is lack of sensation on our emotional body because its energy is absent. We register perfect equilibrium in the absolute. We have entered the fathomless void of the creation, the source of consciousness and of love.

Duality and Absence of the Emotional Body

Although we have entered the absolute through the emotional dimension, we still experience duality. There is still a portion of the self that has not yet surrendered, which is the awareness in the mental body.

During the present condition, the mental body acknowledges the absence of both the ethereal and the emotional bodies. We experience an energetic fluctuation between the soul and the portion of the mental body that has not surrendered.

If we want to fully register absence, as a nondual condition, it has to be done by completely crossing into the absolute realm through all three soul centers, the ethereal, emotional, and mental, simultaneously.

I will explain that extreme condition in detail during the chapter on the self-realization of universality.

Meanwhile, I want to emphasize that absence is not a cataleptic or suspended condition in which we are lost in an unknown dimension. The experience of the absolute is a conscious condition in which there is always someone—a witness consciousness—acknowledging this event. It means that someone was or is registering that condition and now is telling the story.

Stabilizing the Condition of Absence Through the Emotional Dimension

Similar to the work of the stabilization in the ethereal dimension, we need to continue working to stabilize the emotional body. We need to maintain our effort to master our emotional energy because emotions will not stop influencing us until we cease our physical existence. Keeping that energy under control must be an everyday practice until the last day of our lives. With enough persistence and adequate surrendering practice, we are able to stabilize the emotional energy and abide in the absolute for longer durations.

Abiding in the absolute after crossing the gate through the emotional dimension requires an advanced degree of spiritual evolution. In fact, we cannot abide in there as human beings. We need to consciously transcend the emotional human condition to be in there at all. Hence, we need to surrender. Only as souls can we abide in the void of the absolute. We need to fully relinquish the emotional body to register it. Nothing related to our human condition can reside in that dimension.

When we fully surrender, we reverse the flow of emotional energy and send it back towards its point of origin outside the physical body. We deplete the energetic field of the emotional soul center by fully surrendering. This is a temporary condition that allows us to register the beyond.

Don't be concerned. We are still alive in the physical dimension and the emotional energy will reappear at the end of the meditation session, bringing us back into the human condition.

For instance, when entering the absolute through the emotional body we may find fluctuation between the final stages of the pure and healed emotional body and the absolute condition. The fluctuation can be a subtle shift between the two conditions because our emotional body is looking for a reference on its actual location. It is a common situation because we are used to being with our emotional body and not absent from it. The nonexistence of our emotional body is unusual for us.

Since we are not attuned to abiding in absence within this dimension, if we want to stabilize it, we have to practice. Continuously surrendering and establishing the boundaries of our emotional condition helps us distinguish the experience of emotional energy from its absence. We need to find equilibrium within the condition of absence in such a way that there are not fluctuations of emotional energy while we are remaining conscious.

We can safely try entering the mental body and continuing our spiritual evolution only after stabilizing the condition of absence. Achieving absence can require a long journey of meditation practice, so be patient and one day it will arrive.

Chapter 13

MASTERING THE MENTAL BODY

In this chapter, I will discuss the purification of the third soul center, which relates to the embodiment of the soul in the mental body. The experience of the mental body during this stage in the self-realization of individuality is slightly different than the awakening of awareness that occurs during the self-realization of personality. This time, as you meditate, you enter the mental body to complete its purification and receive the full illumination of the soul.

You require a deeper stage of meditation to purify the mental body and need to fully surrender both the ethereal and emotional bodies before proceeding to access the mental body. You have to ensure that you do not detect any interference from other centers that may affect your current condition. After you learn how to control your emotional and ethereal energy, there only is a small amount of residual energy coming from these dimensions of your being that could affect the mental body.

The transition, when entering the mental body from the absolute during this final stage, is a subtle process. It is an act in which you, as a soul, approach the mental body for further purification.

And let us remember that the mind cannot purify itself. It needs something more powerful to do this.

It is the presence of the soul illuminating the mental body from the absolute that stabilizes your mental energy. During this event, the soul observes and guides the mind while the mental body acknowledges the presence of the soul.

Purifying the mental body involves the dedicated teamwork of mind and soul. It is not just a simple act in which the mental body is observing itself. It is dual exercise between the soul and the energetic field of the mental body.

You are now in a condition where the mind surrenders and allows the soul to guide it. You surrender mental energy to create a link between your personality and the soul. You are attuning your relative consciousness (awareness) to the consciousness of the soul. As I mentioned before, the mental soul center has three components: The throat, third eye, and crown chakras. Energetic recognition of these three components is necessary to purify the energy field of the mental body.

Meditation to Purify your Mental Body

The first step of the purification process is to recognize the flow of energy within your mental body to the surrender it.

Surrendering the mental body energy during this stage is relatively easy compared to the surrendering process we previously discussed. There is a now a minimal amount of energy influencing the mental body since the ethereal and emotional bodies have both already been purified.

Since the throat chakra functions as a transition point between the emotional and mental bodies; you can approach and enter your mental body coming either directly at it from the emotional body or from the condition of absence in the absolute realm.

You can start observing the energy flow at the base of the mental body—in the throat chakra located in the neck—where you register some fluctuations of energy.

The energy flow within the mental body is similar to airwaves. Within the mental body the energy flows in two directions. Looking at it from an upright position, the flow goes down from the crown chakra to the third eye chakra and them to the throat chakra at the front side and inside the headspace. The flow goes up from the throat chakra to the third eye chakra and them to the crown chakra at the back side and inside of the headspace.

You may begin approaching the flow of upward-moving energy with your attention in this area and travel with it to enter your mental body. When you access that energy, you start becoming one with its flow.

SURRENDERING MENTAL BODY ENERGY

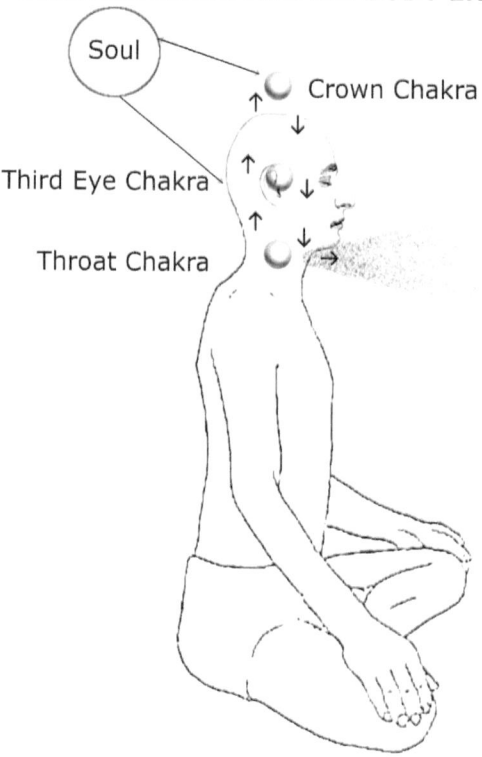

As you breathe, with each inhalation you can increase the flow of energy going upwards to your third eye chakra, and with each exhalation, you may surrender unwanted energy that is blocking movement in your energetic system and send this with the downwards flow to the throat chakra. With each out breath, you also release any arising thoughts and continue flowing upwards Gradually, you arrive at the third eye chakra located just above the base of the skull and stay there.

Every instant that we surrender, we are further developing our capacity to rest and quietly transforming our entire mental body into a clear and silent space.

After continuous surrender, and without any rush, we finally clarify the mind and begin expanding into an immense ocean of transparence. This state is the clarity of the purified mental body, which is fully illuminated by the soul.

Now, the flow of energy within the mental body becomes very slow because the only mental activity occurring is recognition of the presence of the soul. There is no activity in the emotional, physical, and ethereal bodies because their energies are in a state of absence.

When you do this meditation for yourself, you will observe how you are allowing your soul to take the command of your mental body; however, your mental body has not yet fully surrendered because you are still sensing the soul within your human existence. As I mentioned before, at this stage of purification, we only feel the presence of the soul within the mental body because both the ethereal and emotional bodies are fully surrendered to it. When you reach this step in your mediation, you will be abiding in the clarity of a high stabilized mental body.

Hang out here for as long as you like and enjoy experiencing pure subjectivity without any interference while acknowledging the presence of the soul.

The presence of the soul reflected in the clarity of your mental body without the influence of the emotional and ethereal bodies is pure consciousness however since you are experiencing consciousness through your mind, we call it pure awareness. This is a more advanced experience of the mental body than you will have had during the awakening of awareness. You are experiencing the maximum degree of purification within the mental body, which is accompanied by a continuous recognition of "I am."

Once you have stabilized this condition, you will acquire mastery over the mental body. You can learn to control the mental body by transcending external influences. The presence of the soul within your purified mental body is the one that fully interprets your identity. If you are successful on this step, it means that you have embodied the soul within your mental body.

Chapter 14

UNIFICATION OF THE THREE CENTERS OF THE SOUL

The self-realization of individuality needs one final step beyond the purification of the mental body. That step is the unification of the three soul centers with the soul. Unification represents the maximum spiritual condition of purification that it is possible to experience in the human body as human beings with an embodied soul. Unification established with a soul-embodied personality.

Remember, our objective is embodying the soul. Fully embodying the soul allows us to experience a transparent, purified self. Unity is the end result of a maturation process that has been accomplished through all the meditations you've done thus far.

In previous chapters, we discussed how to isolate and fully surrender each of the centers of the soul in an individual form with the exception of the mental body, which fully surrenders its awareness later on. For the mental body, surrender occurs during the self-realization of universality and after the unification process that will be described in this chapter.

Meditation to Obtain a Unified Form

Let us see how we need to progress through all the centers of the soul to obtain a unified form.

This time, as you meditate, you need to surrender through all the soul centers starting with the ethereal soul center, but without entering the absolute. Instead, continue flowing upwards from one center to the next one above it and embodying the soul as you go. By doing so, you are embodying the soul into the ethereal, emotional, and mental bodies almost simultaneously and postponing the access of absolute to a different stage.

During the unification of the three soul centers, you will be dissolving the boundaries between them so that you can experience them as if they are one larger energetic field. You need to check that they are acting in a "fluid" manner without any obstructions among them.

In the past, you could have found stagnant energy or blockages in them, but after having thoroughly prepared yourself, you now should be able to perceive a free flow of energy among all three of them.

The most important thing is to experience a free flow of energy through the main points of surrender to the soul from within each soul center. In the ethereal body, the main point of surrender is the root chakra. In the emotional body, it is the solar plexus chakra. In the mental body, it is the throat chakra.

Despite dissolving boundaries between the three centers of the soul, we are not moving our mental body into our emotional body or our ethereal body. The centers function as a unified field but also retain distinct identities. We are not shifting their positions, only verifying that the gates of the centers are open and allowing for the free exchange energy between adjacent ones.

Specifically, two gates are open. We open the throat chakra to let energy flow freely between the mental and emotional bodies. We open the solar plexus chakra to allow energy to flow freely between the emotional and ethereal bodies.

You can check the unification of your three centers during each meditation practice you do by sensing the energy flowing within the three soul centers while you are surrendering. Begin by surrendering the ethereal body until you reach the condition of "being," and continue progressing upward through your emotional and mental bodies as best you can.

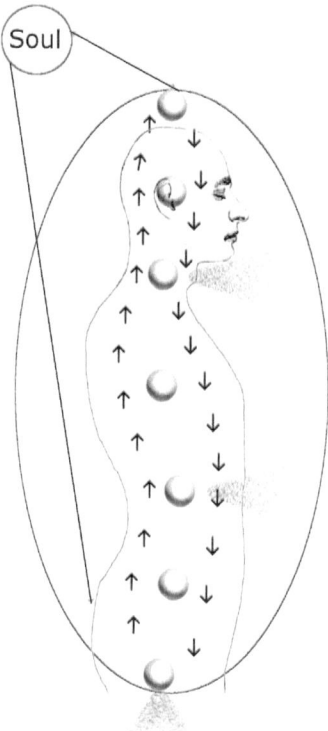

UNITY OF THE SOUL CENTERS WITH FREE FLOW OF ENERGY

The experience of surrendering will be different for individual practitioners and depend on their measure of spiritual evolution. That said, within the ethereal body the perception of the flow is similar to water flowing throughout a network of channels within the body and going down into the ground.

Within the emotional body, the sensation of energy changes because it is subtler. Here, the energy flow is similar to steam escaping and being depleted through the solar plexus.

And within the mental body, the impression of energy is similar to airwaves dissipating through the throat because it is even subtler.

The flow of energy through the centers will become slower and slower until the energy entirely disappears, leaving us in a complete resting state where we are abiding as a unified pure self.

During the unification process, you will be widening your existence in all directions. At the end, you will be immersed in the unlimited sparklingly clear water of a transparent ocean. This sensation is a sign of the presence of the soul within our three bodies integrated as one.

Your personality has transformed all together into a pure self with the illumination of the soul. The purified self of the three centers have embodied "I am." This is the highest degree of the soul evolution that you can perceive within the human body. This is the culmination of the self-realization of individuality. It is the fusion of the three centers with "I am."

Your soul evolves through innumerable incarnations as you allow its evolution as a human being.

You, as a soul, naturally follows the laws of the universal source. When you are a fully embodied soul, you are in a dimension of presence within a purified human self. The three aspects of your soul are united with the three aspects of the pure self: mind, emotions, and body. This is how you may embody the one that allows you to think, feel, and exist within the physical dimension. You experience the unity between your soul and your purified self.

PART FOUR

THE SELF-REALIZATION OF UNIVERSALITY

Chapter 15

THE QUEST FOR THE ABSOLUTE

The self-realization of universality is the realization of the soul and the beginning of its evolution into the absolute dimension.

If you have done the meditations in the preceding chapters successfully before you arrived here, then you have evolved through deep stages of surrender and surpassed pairs and polarities. You have learned to sense your soul within your ethereal, emotional, and mental bodies and, finally, you have consolidated your earthly existence with your soul into one identity. Now, your soul wants you to evolve into more advanced stages of development; and this time, it will allow you to recognize yourself only as a soul without the constraints of the body and the human identity.

If you have not reached this point in your meditations yet, please read this material aspirationally. It may inspire you to redouble your commitment to your spiritual development.

Once you are capable of registering only as a soul, you are able to merge with the universal source and have self-realization of universality. When the soul merges within the source, it is absorbed into the uncreated and its identity establishes itself in absence rather than in presence. This event is as if the soul were someone beforehand, but afterwards is no one anymore. During this process, the soul returns to its place of origin and registers only as consciousness within the universal source.

With the self-realization of universality, you fulfill the main purpose of your existence. During this stage, you reclaim your origin and become free from coming back once you die from the physical existence. You become a master of wisdom within the light of the universal source and begin functioning from your soul.

The self-realization of universality has three important stages. The first is surrendering awareness until you register only as a soul. The second is merging with the universal source. And the third is learning how to function as an individual with the light of the universal source in your daily life.

Through the self-realization of universality, you become whole. you complete the awakening process and merge all the aspects of your existence into your individuality.

Awareness vs. Consciousness

Before going any deeper into the self-realization of universality, I would like to clarify two important concepts directly linked with our spiritual evolution: *awareness* and *consciousness*.

Let us begin with a discussion of awareness. Being aware of something requires the involvement of your physical, emotional, or mental body. Without a mind, emotions, or body, you are unable to experience awareness simply because there is no one present to experience it.

By contrast, consciousness, is different because the source of consciousness lies outside the limits of mind, emotions, and body. Consciousness belongs to the soul.

The self with the body has awareness of something while the soul goes beyond the sense of awareness to register consciousness. It is for this reason that when someone is aware does not necessarily mean that he or she is conscious. Within this book, awareness entirely refers to experience of the soul reflected within the ethereal, emotional, and mental bodies and consciousness strictly applies to the soul.

Awareness is a very important quality, particularly when working within the self-realization of individuality. Without awareness, it would be impossible for you to embody your soul. Now, within the self-realization of universality, the experience of awareness becomes secondary to the experience of consciousness. While you need a body to experience awareness, you do not necessarily need it to register consciousness. In fact, the presence of a strong awareness is a barrier for you to register consciousness.

During the self-realization of universality, if you have a strong awareness, it becomes very difficult to liberate your soul. With intense awareness, you do not want to give up. You do not want to let go because you only want to exist!

During the self-realization of universality, you need to isolate your individuality so that you can register as only a soul. The mind needs to weaken its awareness allowing consciousness to take its place. This is an intricate process that is only possible when you surrender your individuality.

Awakening vs. Samadhi

For the sake of clarity, it is important to differentiate the concepts of *awakening* and *samadhi*.

Awakening is a stage of spiritual maturation in which we undergo fundamental changes within each of our centers of the soul and learn to experience higher conditions of our existence. It is an important phase in which we recognize our pure self as it is being illuminated by the soul.

The stage known as samadhi corresponds to a condition of absence—specifically, the absence of the energy from the centers of the soul and the encounter of the soul with the source of creation.

Through the process of surrendering, we can accomplish both awakening and samadhi; however, it is the depth of surrendering that separates one from the other.

During the stage of awakening, you surrender your personal self to become a purified self with the presence of the soul. Then, during samadhi, you surrender your purified self to realize only as a soul and to merge with the universal source. As you can see, awakening and samadhi are two different albeit interdependent stages.

It is not possible to reach samadhi before awakening because recognizing your real identity is necessary to consciously merge into the absolute.

Awakening implies reversing the flow of ethereal, emotional, and mental energy to purify aspects of the lower self and become a pure self that is capable of embodying the light of the soul.

Samadhi involves transcending the ethereal, emotional, and mental dimensions of existence entirely so that the soul can be in unity with the universal source.

The realization of individuality takes place within the three centers of soul, which function both as sensors to awakening the soul and as portals to access the absolute. The first stages of surrendering facilitate awakening while deeper stages of surrendering provide samadhi.

During awakening, you experience a continuous expansion of each of your soul centers. When transitioning from an awakened condition to a samadhi condition, you are transitioning between presence and absence.

As I have previously discussed in earlier chapters, during a deep phase of surrendering, the first aspect of your individuality capable of accessing the absolute is the energy of the ethereal body. This is followed by the energy of the emotional and mental bodies in turn. As you cross from each condition into the absolute, the transformation of your self-referencing identity reflects your transcendence into a next dimension of existence. At the end, each aspect (or all three aspects) of the soul are in the absolute providing a condition of samadhi.

Chapter 16

SURRENDERING AWARENESS AND LIBERATION

The self-realization of universality represents the evolution of the soul into the source of creation. This advanced stage implies the liberation of the soul from any element of existence. In other words, during this process, you need to surrender your individuality to free your soul from all aspects of the dimension of presence.

It may sound bizarre, but during this process you relinquish everything because within the source of creation there is only room for the soul. It is for this reason that surrendering your individuality is the fulfillment of the journey within the human condition.

The only way for your soul to transcend the dimension of presence is by surrendering the purified self of the mental body, the portion of you that contains the ego sense and at the same time provides you with awareness.

When you surrender the purified self of the mind, the only portion left is the eternal "I am." You begin registering only as a soul and free from the influence of the human condition. It is here that the energy of the soul which was initially flowing into the purified self shifts towards the source of creation.

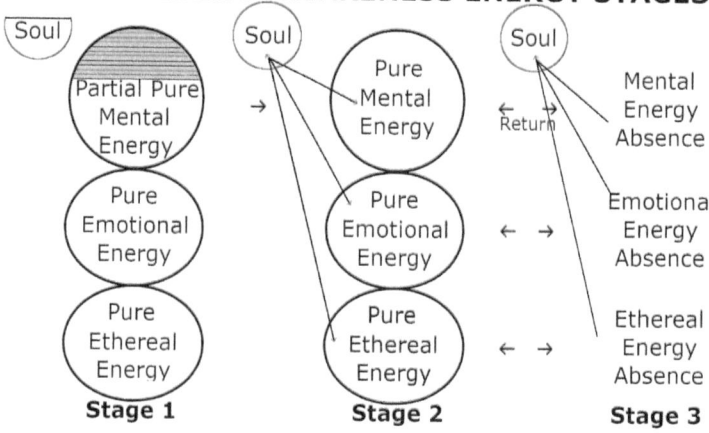

Remember that when you surrender into the absolute through the ethereal and emotional bodies, you also transcend the human condition and register as a soul. However, it is only when you at last move into the absolute through the mental body that you transcend the total influence of the human condition to liberate your soul.

Throughout the process of surrendering awareness (the mental energy), both soul and mind are continuously communicating. This is why the pure self can be aware of the presence of the soul. As you fully surrender the mental body, you suspend this communication briefly, detaching the soul. From then on, there is no one experiencing the presence of the soul within the human existence. The soul has been liberated.

During this shift, each energetic element of the pure self is absorbed within its own source, but you do not die. I am describing a perceptual shift. You are only temporarily releasing the soul from the presence of the human existence.

At the top of the head, which is the location of the physical center known as the crown chakra, you find the gate of communication and turning point between your individuality and your universality. The crown chakra serves a similar function as the root, solar plexus, and throat chakras did within their corresponding bodies. Except this time, at the crown, you find the platform to access the highest human spiritual transformation.

During the transitional stage between individuality and universality, you evolve into the highest level of your mental body. You are at the edge, ready to advance into universal consciousness. When you surrender the mental energy fully, you relinquish awareness and gain access to the gate of universality.

During meditation, while abiding within your purified mental energy, you can experience the illumination of the soul with a sense of pure subjectivity. The awareness of the mental body confirms the source of that illumination: the duality of the soul and the mind! As you transition between soul and mind, you experience the energy of your mental body, at the level of your third eye chakra and registers as a soul projecting from the back of your head.

As you breathe, with each inhalation you begin ascending with the flow upwards to your crown chakra, and with each relaxed exhalation of breath, you continuously surrender your presence, diving from the middle of your mental soul center down into the gate of the throat chakra.

As you continuous surrendering through the throat chakra, there is a subtle shift between you as a soul and you as a pure self of the mental body. One instant, you are the mental body observing, and the next, you register as a soul. The duality is continuous until the action of the mental energy becomes more passive and lets your soul take control. You as a soul begin shifting towards the top of the head while continuously surrendering and depleting your mental energy through the throat chakra. The intervals of cross-reference between the pure self (our mental body) and the soul become longer and longer as you get closer to your crown chakra. You are the pure self surrendering, and then, mere moments later, you are the soul observing the pure self.

When entering the crown chakra, you uncover two dimensions. Above, you find an endlessness universe. Below, you find the purified self. The perception is similar to the union of two funnels. Below you are the created, and above you are the uncreated. When projecting above the crown, you turn into everything, and thus, become nonexistent within the void of the infinite. When projecting below, you become existent and enclosed within limits.

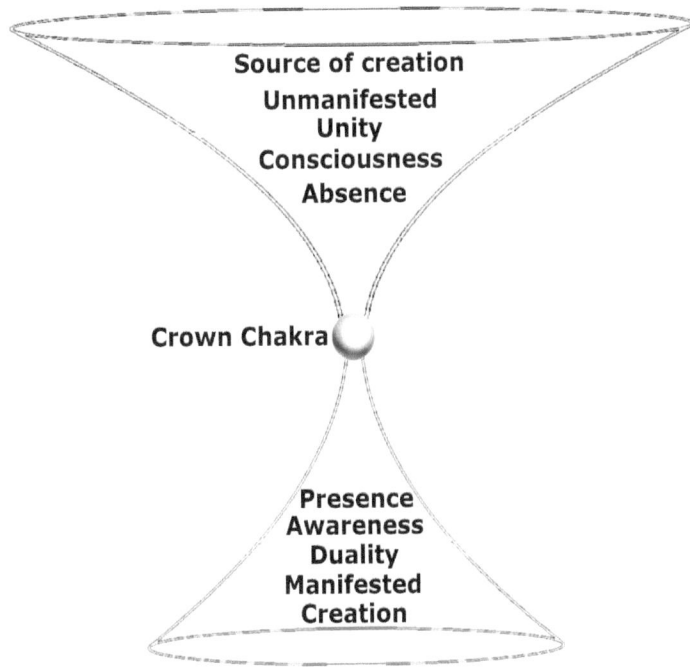

THE FUNNELS OF THE CROWN CHAKRA

Chapter 17

MERGING INTO THE UNIVERSAL SOURCE

As you continue deep in meditation at the crown chakra, the gate of universality opens and you begin to be absorbed into a vast universe. As you ascend, you start the mission of relinquishing your individuality by letting go of any traces of your existence. Your individuality begins vanishing, allowing you to merge with the luminosity of the source.

Above the crown chakra, the luminosity of the source increases while the awareness of the individuality dissolves. The crown chakra is the boundary in which the soul shifts into pure consciousness. It is the convergence point between the human aspect and universality.

Once you attain this condition, you can see two dimensions with different receptors. Perceptions below the crown chakra relate to awareness within your individuality. Perceptions above the crown chakra specifically relate to pure consciousness, the energy of the soul.

When you go above the crown chakra, there are no more cross-reference checks between the soul and the mind. The mind enters total repose and temporarily ceases its inquiries of presence yielding to the soul. The soul continues upwards, expanding within the transparent luminosity of the source.

During this stage, the flow of energy from the awareness of the purified self is depleted through your throat chakra while surrendering and you begin registering only your soul within the source of creation. Your soul still remains linked to your isolated body during the condition of absence. You become only your soul because the energetic flow of your body enters into a period of restfulness during which you do not experience any sensations.

After leaving the crown chakra and merging your soul with the absolute, you begin establishing a direct link of communication among the source of creation, the soul, and your individuality. The process of merging your soul with the absolute is known as the *transcendental state* or simply *transcendence*.

Transcending is going beyond the human condition and arriving into the perfection of your original source. You, self-referencing as the soul, are surpassing the earthly dimension to enter into absence with all the wisdom you bring along.

The transcendental state corresponds to a condition in which the awareness of the human dimension is pulled into complete surrender to allow the soul to merge with the absolute. This is a subtle stage in which we transcend into absence and universality.

For contrast, let's say that the self-realization of individuality is a condition of the soul in unity with the pure self while the self-realization of universality is a condition of the soul in unity with the source at the absolute.

During the transcendental state, you go beyond your human individuality. Your soul's liberation from the confines of the human condition allows your nonlocal sense of self to move into a boundless space of universal intelligence free from individuality.

While in a transcendental state, you go beyond the dimension that follows the law of complementary pairs and polarities (up/down, dark/light, in/out, me/not-me), surpassing the perceptual limits of gender and any other kind of dualism.

Your transition into the abode of the unmanifested is a progression into a fathomless zone of absence, a realm of the uncreated, a dimension of reality without polarities, and a source of creation. It is an evolution into the abode of universal subjectivity and pure consciousness where the soul blends with the universal wisdom. In this dimension, there is no experience and no experiencers. There is no personality or mind involved, no presence, no activity, and no time, only pure consciousness.

If you want to be able to perceive universal wisdom, you need to complete your earthly evolution. Any ties related to desire, attachments, or subconscious tendencies will keep pulling your soul away from you. It is only when you feel peace that you can let go of your earthly awareness.

To enter into the realm of universal wisdom, you need to become your soul. But remember that the soul is only linked to your human essence; it does not reside within the same dimension as your human self. For this reason, you cannot completely realize your soul before transcending your human awareness—your human mind. If you want to become your soul, you need to join the energy of the soul (consciousness) and merge into the field of universal intelligence.

The result of the transcendental state is the condition of samadhi. In Sanskrit, *samadhi* literally means "putting together"!

During the self-realization of universality, you put together your soul with the universal source (aka the absolute).

Following the definition above then, you may encounter three kinds of samadhi, depending on the level of your inner development. Samadhi through the ethereal energy, samadhi through the emotional energy and samadhi through the mental energy or samadhi of the absolute.

Samadhi of the absolute is an advanced condition, which happens when your purified soul centers fully surrender, allowing your soul to enter the realm of absence.

You can register samadhi of the absolute only through your soul and never through bodily sensations. Samadhi of the absolute involves the total surrender of awareness because the human condition is too gross to enter into that subtlest of dimensions.

This is the progression of samadhi you have been studying throughout this book and have been or will be practicing in steps and stages going forward.

1. Samadhi through the ethereal energy. By fully surrendering your ethereal energy, your soul enters the absolute through

the being condition of the soul. It is the unity of the soul with the universal source of creation aspect within the absolute.

2. Samadhi through the emotional energy. By fully surrendering your purified emotional energy, your soul enters the absolute through the divine condition of the soul. It is the unity of the soul with the universal source of love aspect in the absolute.
3. Samadhi through the mental energy or samadhi of the absolute. By fully surrendering your mental energy, your soul enters the absolute through the awareness condition of the soul. It is the unity of the soul with the universal source of consciousness aspect in the absolute.

Samadhi stages are superimposed on one another. Refer to the dimensions of the soul explained in Chapter 2. This means that to enter samadhi of the absolute you need to have entered samadhi through both the emotional and ethereal conditions. Similar to enter samadhi through emotional energy you need to have entered though the ethereal energy too.

During samadhi of the absolute, you, as a soul, register union with the universal source in a condition of absence.

There is a considerable difference between experiencing the soul reflected on your body and mind and registering you only as a soul without a body. During samadhi of the absolute, you do not experience your pure self. You only register your soul resting in the realm of absence.

Within the self-realization of universality, you register samadhi of the absolute. You register emptiness or absence because you are abiding in the dimension of the uncreated.

As you can see, samadhi of the absolute is an inexplicable nondual condition, which contravenes the normal human understanding of the world. Simply, there is no access for human perception there.

During samadhi of the absolute, you may register endlessness and at the same time nothingness. You simultaneously abide in the fathomless immensity of everywhere and nowhere.

Contrary to the dimension of the soul, which is boundless and infinite, the human dimension has boundaries and limitations. Within the human dimension, you can only ever be in a single place at once. Within the soul dimension, you can remain ubiquitous and absent.

The condition of emptiness I describe is much more than the simple definition of nothingness you could imagine occurring within a human context. It is the nothingness of unmanifested potential, the state of nonpresence, and the void of existence. It is a perfect vacuum of absence because the relativity of time and space is completely stopped.

Reaching this state through meditation is tricky. Your purified body is not conscious of the passage of time or its presence in space because it is registering only as a soul does. Samadhi of the absolute transcends the relativity of the creation because we enter the source within the void of the uncreated dimension.

Please forgive me. The writing above is only a crude description of samadhi of the absolute. There are no words to sufficiently explain this condition, particularly because we cannot compare samadhi of the absolute with any other event happening within the created, transient dimension.

Chapter 18

INTEGRATION OF SAMADHI WITHIN YOUR DAILY LIFE

During the first stage of the self-realization of universality, you had to surrender your individuality to gain access to the absolute. Now, within the second stage of the self-realization of universality, you have to come back and integrate your individuality with the soul and the source of creation.

When the soul enters the absolute, it opens a path for individuality to follow; however, it is not possible to infuse your individuality with the energy of your soul or the source before being able to stabilize the soul within the absolute. So, that is the next ability to practice.

Some traditions call this capacity for merging our souls and stabilizing with the absolute the stage of *ascension*. The soul is not embodied here; it remains in its dimension without forming a separate identity. But our individuality at last becomes a pure expression of the soul.

Acquiring samadhi of the absolute without fluctuation is a good indication that we have prepared the path for direct three-way communication among the source of creation, the soul, and our human individuality.

Merging our individuality with the soul and the absolute is the full realization of universality. The individual becomes responsive to the complete soul's guidance and the realm of the source. The purified self by the point we can accomplish this in our meditation session is a reliable vehicle serving its source and the soul within the physical dimension

Beyond the bliss and peacefulness of the meditation, the beauty of this incredible immersion experience is how your individuality comes back to you infused with your soul and the source of creation. Now, there is an expression of soul in everything you do and how you live. You see life from the perspective of a wise soul.

The personality that existed inside the body before is not in there anymore because your soul has fully transformed it from the source of creation. The mind and, in general, all their preexisting psychological issues have burned away. All emotional imprints from past experiences have expired and are not in effect anymore. It's as if a new person is being born! If this happens to you, people around may be confused by your personality changes.

Only you will know exactly what is happening inside you. After all, you directed every single step of this transformation. You are not the person you used to be! You are different! You are the original you, the genuine you, evolving into new dimensions of your being and following the purpose of your soul. You precisely know the obstacles that you had to overcome to reach this stage of spiritual maturation.

The problem that you may encounter in your daily life is that you cannot live in an isolated state. You still need to interact with others. Your challenge then is learning how to function and thrive after this transformation because your environment can make integration of your new perspective difficult.

It is true. You won't be the same person. People most intimate with you may be the ones who will try the impossible: to get you to revert back to your old condition. They loved your old personality and will not be ready to accept the changes in your behavior.

This is natural. The closer people are to you, the harder it is for them to accept your changes because it means something in their lives will have to shift for them to stay in relationship with you.

The good news, however, is that you will be capable of adjusting your individuality to live in a natural and efficient manner with others and meet them where they are.

When you interact with others, your soul-infused personality is regenerated. However, this time it is different than before because you are relating to others directly from your soul. Your challenge through this process is learning how to interact with people by continuously abiding in your soul.

You just need to take a beat to learn how to interact with others with the wisdom of the soul and from the place of love. You will get there, but it might "take a minute."

Your soul has the wisdom to distinguish when other people are being real with you, and it will expose itself to them only when they are being real in return. Your soul loves all beings but it does not want to linger with others who do not yet have their souls with them.

For instance, very often you encounter people that disrupt your peace. You may wish to avoid people who are very submerged in the material world, lost in their emotions, and or extremely analytical. You may try to disconnect however you still experience them with tender feeling from your soul.

Souls prefer meeting other souls. They choose connecting to other soul-infused people because they want to expand their consciousness and love. If there is no chance for interaction with another soul, the soul elects to leave because it prefers to be alone to enduring painful interactions. The soul always makes the right decision because it acts upon the light of universal consciousness and love.

Our mission in life is to learn to fill our existence with universal consciousness and light. So, stabilizing the condition of samadhi of the absolute within our mundane existence is of extreme importance. But it takes time. After a transitional period, your behavior and lifestyle will become a natural expression of your soul.

To be blunt, we need to stabilize and integrate our inner condition with our individuality in such a way that there is no difference between being seated in meditation and being involved in our normal activities. This integration period is perhaps the most difficult stage of the self-realization of universality.

Integrating samadhi of the absolute with normal activities is not an easy task particularly due to the profound level of absence that we experience during this stage. The challenge here is not only to keep our inner condition intact but to complete any external interaction or activity in a normal and coherent fashion.

Abiding in the beyond and learning how to operate from there now becomes and important stage of your spiritual evolution. You cannot just go into the absolute and remain there while the human body is alive. The soul wants to lead a "normal" life in the human dimension. You cannot become obsessed and sit in meditation ten hours a day to maintain your condition.

At the end, you should be able to maintain your samadhi state without much difference both during meditation and during our daily routines. Once you have a well-established and integrated the samadhi state, you will have truly finished your journey within the constraints of time and space. Your existence will have been transmuted into the essence of your never-ending soul in unity with the light of creation. You will have entered the dimension of the creator, the eternal source of everything in our manifested world. You will be able to recognize it with your transcendental being as a universal self living with consciousness, love, and bliss.

LIST OF DIAGRAMS

The three Soul Centers	Page 18
The Ethereal Body	Page 19
The Emotional Body	Page 20
The Mental Body	Page 21
Dimensions of Reality	Page 24
The Links to Consciousness and Vital Energy	Page 29
Becoming a Conscious Observer	Page 60
Surrendering Ethereal Body Energy	Page 86
Surrendering Ethereal Energy Stages	Page 98
Surrendering Emotional Body Energy	Page 119
Surrendering Emotional Energy Stages	Page 139
Surrendering Mental Body Energy	Page 146
Unity of the Soul Centers with Free Flow Energy	Page 152
Surrendering Awareness Energy Stages	Page 164
The Funnels of the Crown Chakra	Page 167

LIST OF PRACTICES

Becoming a Self-Aware observer	Page 53
Becoming a Conscious Observer	Page 59
The Awakening of Awareness	Page 62
Self-Remembrance and Presence	Page 71
Surrendering Within the Ethereal Body	Page 84
The Experience of Being	Page 90
A Purified Ethereal Body	Page 93
The Absolute Through the Ethereal Dimension	Page 95
Duality Through the Ethereal Dimension	Page 99
Stabilizing Absence Through the Ethereal Dimension	Page 100
Purification of the Emotional Body	Page 106
Allowing Free Flow of Emotions	Page 110
Inner Energetic Work to Purify the Emotional Body	Page 116
Healing the Emotional Body	Page 122
Trust Is the Foundation of Healing	Page 123
Realization of the Heart Chakra	Page 128

Inner Energetic Work to Heal the Emotional Body	Page 135
The Absolute Through the Emotional Dimension	Page 137
Duality and Absence of the Emotional Body	Page 140
Stabilizing Absence Through the Emotional Dimension	Page 141
Mastering the Mental Body	Page 143
Unification of the Three Centers of the Soul	Page 149
The Quest for the Absolute	Page 158
Surrendering Awareness and Liberation	Page 164
Merging into the Universal Source	Page 169
Integration of Samadhi within Your Daily Life	Page 175

REFERENCES

As I was writing the book, I read many wonderful books that influenced my thinking. The ideas that I included from these sources is not a direct duplication of these books' contents. I do not include specific excerpts of the material. However, I would like to acknowledge them as the basis for an in-depth analysis. Without this material, and a dedicated practice of meditation it would have been impossible for me to develop and complete this book.

Also, throughout the book I include descriptions of my personal meditation experiences from periods of seclusion and different retreats, during the years 2012, 2013, and 2014 in Uttarakhand in northern India. I have included analysis or insights drawn from conversations with people who were in retreat with me, as well as from friends. In all cases, their identifying information has been omitted.

Special thanks go to the authors of the wonderful books I list below.

Anadi. *Book of Enlightenment* (Alresford, Hants, U.K.: Mantra Books, 2013).

Bailey, Alice A. *Twenty-Four Books of Esoteric Philosophy*. (New York, N.Y.: Lucis Trust, 1998).

Bryant, Edwin F. & Patañjali. *Yoga sutras of Patanjali*. (New York, N.Y.: North Point Press, 2009).

Eswaran, Eknath. *The Bhagavad Gita* (Tomales, CA.: Nilgiri Press, 2007).

Eswaran, Eknath. *The Upanishads* (Tomales, CA.: Nilgiri Press, 2007).

Johnson, Jerry A. *Daoist Alchemy: Nei Gong & Wei Gong Training* (Pacific Grove, CA.: The International Institute of Medical Qigong Publishing House, 2013).

Krishnamurti, Jiddu. *Krishnamurti: Reflections on the Self* (Chicago, IL.: Open Court Publishing, 1998).

Krishnamurti, Jiddu. *The Book of Life: Daily Meditations with Krishnamurti* (New York, N.Y.: HarperOne, 1995).

Lin, Derek. *Tao Te Ching: Annotated & Explained* (Woodstock, VT.: SkyLight Paths Publishing, 2006).

Nisargadatta, Maharaj. *I Am That: Talks with Sri Nisargadatta Maharaj*, translated by Maurice Frydman (Durham, N.C.: Acorn Press, 1999).

Pregadio, Fabrizio. *Foundations of Internal Alchemy: The Taoist Practice of Neidan* (Mountain View, CA.: Golden Elixir Press, 2012).

Saraswati, Satyananda. *A Systematic Course In The Ancient Tantric Techniques Of Yoga & Kriya* (Munger, Bihar, India.: Yoga Publications Trust, Ganga Darshan, 1981)

Venkatesananda, Swami. *Vasistha's Yoga* (Albany, N.Y.: State University of New York Press, 1993).

ABOUT THE AUTHOR

For over thirty years, Fernando A. Obando has been studying spirituality and practicing meditation. While he is not aligned with any specific religion or tradition, his engineering skills along with his spiritual mindset have inspired him to teach the processes of self-realization in a more comprehensive way.

His wide experience and attitude within different areas of engineering, and spirituality has encouraged many people to improve their human capabilities and extend the range of their human spirit.

He teaches a life-changing, progressive series of meditations that will help you to clear your energy centers and make room for the soul to enter your body as a lived experience.

Embodying Your Soul is his first book on meditation and spiritual self-realization. He also completed a study about the vibratory effect of specific notes produced by Tibetan singing bowls on the chakra system.

Fernando lives in Oakville, Ontario, with his wife, Janet.

Share Your Experience!

I value your feedback, and so do your fellow readers. Reviews you leave on your eBook store help more people find and enjoy the books you love. So spread the word, write a review, and share your experience!

NOTES

NOTES

NOTES

NOTES

www.ingramcontent.com/pod-product-compliance
Lightning Source LLC
Chambersburg PA
CBHW022042160426
43209CB00002B/40